AMAZING
ATHLETES
AMAZING
MOMENTS

STEVE RIACH

AMAZING ATHLETES AMAZING MOMENTS

by Steve Riach

Design © 2005 Hallmark Licensing, Inc.

Text © 2005 by Steve Riach and/or VisionQuest Communications Group Inc.

Visit us on the Web at www.Hallmark.com.

On the Cover and above, from left: Runners © *Alan Thornton/Stone/Getty Images*; Orel Hershiser *Jonathan Daniel /Allsport/Getty Images*; Women's bobsled team © *Reuters/CORBIS*; Michelle Akers *Tim Sloan/AFP/Getty Images*

On the Cover: Brett Favre *Don Emmert/AFP/Getty Images*; Basketball *Doug Pensinger/Getty Images*

On the Title Page: Brett Favre *Don Emmert/AFP/Getty Images*; David Robinson *Matt Rourke/ AFP/ Getty Images*

Printed in the USA   First Edition, March 2005   ISBN: 1-59530-036-8

10 9 8 7 6 5 4 3 2 1

BOK2056

ABOUT THE AUTHOR

Steve Riach is president and cofounder of VisionQuest Communications Group, Inc., a Dallas-based media company. He is an award-winning producer, writer, and director of numerous television, film, and video projects, and is one the the nation's foremost creators of virtuous and positive-themed sports content. Steve's programs have been seen on ESPN, FOX Sports, NBC, PAX-TV, and a variety of broadcast and cable television outlets. He is also the principal behind the creative vision for the *Heart of a Champion*™ brand of sports-related programs and properties. His start in sports media came as an on-air personality, hosting national television and radio programming.

Steve is also the cofounder of the *Heart of a Champion Foundation,* a nonprofit organization devoted to producing materials designed to teach character and virtue to children. Steve is creator and author of the foundation's innovative *Heart of a Champion*™ *Character Development Program,* a tool for the character education of students in schools across America.

A former college baseball player at the University of the Pacific, Steve also speaks to school groups, youth agencies, corporations, sports organizations, and churches.

ACKNOWLEDGEMENTS

Amazing Athletes, Amazing Moments is the result of years of research and documentation. As with projects of this magnitude, I received much help from many caring people. I would like to thank the following:

My wife, Wendy, and children, Kristen, Josh, Elissa, and Anna, who have unselfishly given me their constant love and support and allowed me the necessary quiet time to write.

My research aide for this book, Nelson Staats, who again did a wonderful job in the numerous hours he spent researching facts and chasing down information late at night.

My good friends Dr. Lance Rawlings and Brad Thomas, with whom I seem to be forever trading stories like those found in this book and laughing like kids at the memories of these moments.

My mother and father, Joan and Tom Riach, who first instilled in me a love of people, sports, competition, and virtue.

John Humphrey, my business partner at VisionQuest, who has been supportive throughout the process.

Harold Reynolds, James Brown, and Clark Kellogg, each of whom at one time or another during the course of our relationship has inspired concepts for a book such as this.

Joe Gibbs, Nolan Ryan, Pat Summerall, Larry Nelson, and Darrell Waltrip, some of the finest men in all of sports, who, through involvement in my previous books, have demonstrated their desire to have a positive influence on our culture.

The Board of Directors of the *Heart of a Champion Foundation*, for their commitment to seeing sports stories utilized to help shape character in young people all across America.

And Todd Hafer at Hallmark, who believed in this book series and was responsible for it becoming a reality.

Thanks, you all!

Steve Riach

The IOC honored John Stephen Akwhari in Sydney in 2000 for his courageous finish in Mexico City in 1968. Hamish Blair /Allsport/Getty Images

AMAZING COURAGE

FINISHING STRONG
JOHN STEPHEN AKHWARI

The year was 1968. The place was Mexico City, site of the 1968 Summer Olympic Games. It happened late one night in the main track and field stadium.

Out of the cold darkness, John Stephen Akhwari from Tanzania entered the stadium. He hobbled slowly and unsteadily. Pain filled his every step. Blood ran down his bandaged leg. His dreams of Olympic glory had long since faded into the shadows of the night.

More than an hour earlier, the winner of the Olympic marathon had already been declared. The other finishers began streaming across the line shortly thereafter. By the time Akhwari approached the stadium, only a few spectators remained in their seats. There was no cheering, no flag waving. Yet the lone runner pressed on.

As he neared the Olympic Stadium, word circulated that there was one runner still struggling to complete the 26.2-mile course. Other Olympians and spectators quickly came back to the stadium to watch the scene unfold. The stadium lights flickered back on. Akhwari entered the stadium and began to wearily pound out his final lap around the track. As he neared the finish line, the small crowd that had gathered began to roar with appreciation. They stood and cheered the lone runner all the way to the finish line. After crossing the white stripe, an exhausted Akhwari nearly collapsed. Yet in his anguish, he managed to stay on his feet and acknowledge the faithful few who had witnessed his final steps.

After it was all over, a reporter asked Akhwari why he had not retired from the race, as he had fallen so far back and had no chance of winning.

Akhwari seemed confused by the question but finally

answered. "My country did not send me 5,000 miles to Mexico City to start the race," he said. "They sent me 5,000 miles to finish the race."

Chris, Stefanie, Madison, and Noah Spielman. Time Life Pictures/Getty Images

AMAZING SACRIFICE

CHRIS SPIELMAN
#1 TEAMMATE

Chris Spielman knows what it's like to take a hit. As a star middle linebacker for three NFL teams, he was one of the league's hardest hitters in a career that spanned 11 seasons. But even this ferocious tackler was not prepared for the emotional hit he took in 1998, his penultimate year in the league. It was then that Spielman's wife, Stefanie, a former model, was stricken with cancer.

Just one year earlier, Spielman had come face to face with football mortality, suffering a neck injury that required surgery and threatened to end his career at the age of 32. But the competitive fires still burned in Spielman, and the former Ohio State All-American was not ready to give up. He planned on a comeback with the Cleveland Browns in 1998. He prepared to show the NFL he was the same player who had been selected to the Pro Bowl four times as a Buffalo Bill and Detroit Lion. What he didn't plan on was having his wife fight cancer at the same time.

In July of 1998, after Stefanie suffered a miscarriage, tests revealed a precancerous tumor in her right breast. An ensuing mammogram and biopsy showed she needed a mastectomy. During the mastectomy, doctors found the cancer had spread to her lymph nodes, demanding further surgery and months of chemotherapy. Spielman made what was for him a quick and easy decision. He abandoned his comeback plans and stayed home to care for his wife and their 4-year-old daughter and 2-year-old son. He committed to sharing the rigors of recovery with Stefanie and to becoming the primary caregiver for the children. "I knew in my heart it was the right thing to do," Spielman said. "We take our wedding vows very seriously."

None of this sat well with Stefanie, who attempted to persuade her husband to go back to football. "I knew how much he wanted to play," she said. "I knew how excited he was about returning to football. I didn't want to be the reason he didn't get to reach that goal."

Spielman heard his wife's plea, but he heard his heart even louder. He gave up football. He had always talked about qualities like responsibility and concern for others. Now he had a chance to show those character qualities in action to his wife and children.

He made breakfast, bathed the children, dispensed their cold medicine, and took them to preschool. He helped them get dressed and took care of their daily needs. He built a Barbie doll house and repaired bicycle tires. He proved himself an All-Pro Parent. He also took Stefanie to all of her chemotherapy appointments. When Stefanie lost her hair during chemotherapy, Chris showed his support by shaving his head. "I don't know what I would have done without him being there," said Stefanie.

Early in 1999, the Spielmans received welcome news: Stefanie's chemotherapy treatments were over, and she appeared to be cancer free and ready to resume a normal life. Later, doctors officially classified her as being in remission.

"When you go through something like we've gone through," Spielman reflects, "it's not a cliché—you really learn to appreciate every day."

Eugenio Monti, 1968 STAFF/AFP/Getty Images

EUGENIO MONTI
SPORTSMANSHIP PERSONIFIED

The 1964 Olympic Winter Games in Innsbruck, Austria, became the site of one of the greatest displays of sportsmanship the world of sports has ever seen. It was there that bobsledding legend Eugenio Monti showed the world what the true spirit of competition is all about.

The bobsled competition looked to be one of the most highly competitive events in all of the games. In the four-man portion of the competition, the hometown Austrians and the Italians, led by Monti, emerged as clear favorites for the gold medal. The Canadian team was expected to compete for the bronze, with an outside chance of finishing higher. But an amazing story unfolded that would forever mark the landscape of Olympic competition.

On their run in the first heat, the Canadian team broke the Olympic record and held a substantial lead (in bobsled terms) of half a second over the rest of the field. However, on that record-setting run the Canadians encountered a problem. Their sled went into the last turn too fast, hit the ice wall, and damaged the axle. If they couldn't fix it before the next heat, they would be disqualified.

Monti did not want to win the event unless he was able to race against each team at its best—and on equal terms. Fifteen minutes before their next run, the Canadian team's Victor Emery reached the top of the track—only to find his sled upside down. In an incredible act of sportsmanship, the Italians had taken the sled apart and Monti's mechanics were fixing it. With Monti's help, the Canadians were able not only to race, but also to stay in the lead and win the gold. Monti and his team had to settle for the bronze.

Later, in the two-man bobsled event, Monti displayed his character once again. On his first run, Great Britain's Tony Nash recorded the fastest time of the competition. But the bolt attaching the sled's runners to the vehicle's shell had sheared. Monti, who was at the top of the course and about

Eugenio Monti leads the Italian bobsled team at the Grenoble, France Olympics.
© Bettmann/CORBIS

to steer the Italian team's sled down the track when he learned of the incident, said, "Get an Englishman and a spanner to the finish, and they can have my bolt." Monti even offered to withdraw from the race if it was the only way he could loan Nash his bolt. True to his word—and ignoring questioning from puzzled Italian journalists— Monti had the bolt from his sled removed and sent back up the hill to the start line, where it was quickly attached to Nash's sled just in time for his run. Once again, Monti's actions proved heroic for his opponents. The team of Nash and Robin Dixon took home the gold for Great Britain.

Again, Monti won the bronze.

When the games were over, Monti was honored for his amazing display of character with the first Pierre de Coubertin Award for Sportsmanship. But not everyone was happy about Monti's respect for his competitors. He was viciously attacked in the Italian newspapers but nevertheless remained steadfast. "Nash didn't win because I gave him the bolt," he explained. "He won because he had the fastest run."

Monti eventually won his gold medal — at age 40. At the 1968 Grenoble Winter Olympic Games, he took the gold in both the two-man and four-man bobsled events. He completed his storied career with six Olympic medals — two gold and two bronze, along with two silvers he earned at the 1956 Olympics in Cortina, Italy. Monti also won nine world championships and gained the nickname "Il Rosso Volante," or The Red Flyer. Recently, award-winning Olympic historian and filmmaker Bud Greenspan, in partnership with General Motors, honored Monti as the 3rd-Greatest Winter Olympian (in any sport) of all time. "Eugenio Monti is deserving of the title as the Greatest Bobsled Driver in history," said Greenspan. "His career was significant, and his gesture of friendship and good sportsmanship in 1964 has been an inspiration for all who

compete at the Olympic Games."

His respect for his competitors and his willingness to put others first earned Eugenio Monti a prominent place in Olympic history. He represented sportsmanship at its best by pursuing victory with honor.

Vonetta Flowers and Jill Bakken at Salt Lake City, 2002 © Reuters/CORBIS

VONETTA FLOWERS

The 2002 Winter Olympic Games provided a dramatic story in the women's bobsled competition, combining a historic finish with a triumphant display of integrity. Team USA-1, led by driver Jean Racine and longtime push-mate Jen Davidson, had won the World Cup titles during the previous two seasons and seemed a lock for the gold medal. During the year leading up to the games, the pair approached celebrity status, appearing on television shows and commercials. If they were able to earn Olympic gold, book deals and product endorsements would follow. But two months prior to the games, Racine decided to part with Davidson, replacing her with a bigger, stronger push-mate (former collegiate track star Gea Johnson). The duo set track records during the Olympic Trials, and the international media asserted they were certain to take the gold.

Lost in the excitement was the USA-2 team of driver Jill Bakken and pusher Vonetta Flowers. Like Johnson, Alabama native Flowers was a former college track star. Still, few thought this team had a chance to medal, much less compete for gold—except Vonetta Flowers.

At a routine practice four days prior to the event, Johnson pulled a hamstring. Racine became worried about her chances and decided to do something about it. "I wasn't going to let anything stop me from trying to win a medal," Racine said of her dilemma. She decided to try to persuade Flowers to switch teams. Just two days before the race, Racine called Flowers with her proposition, telling Flowers it was her only chance to win gold. "She said, basically, that she didn't think Jill would be ready, and she wanted me to push for her," Flowers said. "She asked me if I would leave Jill and compete with her."

Flowers told Racine that she had come to Salt Lake City to ride with Bakken and knew she could not turn her back on her friend and teammate, even if it cost her a

chance for the gold medal. "I told her no," said Flowers. "I told her I was loyal to Jill, that I thought we had a chance to win a gold medal."

On the track two days later, a disappointed Racine and her injured partner Johnson logged the third-worst time in the first heat. Meanwhile, Bakken and Flowers staggered the field by racing to the fastest time of the day: 48.81 seconds. They were 0.29 seconds ahead of their closest competition—a huge margin in bobsledding. With such a large lead, all USA-2 had to do was stay on the track and they would take home the gold. Bakken and Flowers not only stayed on track; they completed a wild and remarkably swift ride in the second heat to finish .29 seconds ahead of Germany 1 and .38 in front of Germany 2. Racine and Johnson finished fifth. Flowers and Bakken won the gold medal.

"All those years when I was running track, I dreamed of someday competing in the Olympics and winning a medal," Flowers said. "Whoever would have thought that it would happen one day on a mountain covered with snow —and me in a sled?"

In victory, Flowers made history. She became the first African-American athlete from any country to win a gold

Vonetta Flowers   Matthew Stockman/Allsport/Getty Images

medal in the 78-year history of the Winter Olympics. "I don't really know what to say about being the first African-American athlete to win a gold medal," said Flowers. "It's an honor, and I hope it gives other African-American boys and girls an opportunity to give winter sports a try."

More than making history, Flowers became a model of integrity who refused to sacrifice her honor for what seemed like her best chance to win. In the end, she won both the medal and the admiration of a nation for her display of character. "What can I say," said Flowers, moved to tears at a postrace press conference. "This is just awesome. This is a dream come true for me. I feel very blessed.

"Jill and I tried to stay out of the soap opera. A lot of people saw us as the 'other team.' We wanted to come here and prove them wrong. We're no longer the other team. We're *the* team. I'm so proud of the way the two of us were able to work together to achieve victory."

Laura Wilkinson in the 10-meter competition, Sydney, 2000
Shaun Botterill /Allsport/Getty Images

AMAZING OVERCOMERS

LAURA WILKINSON

L aura Wilkinson has always appreciated a good comeback story. "Triumphs over tragedies—I love stories like that," she explained after her performance at the 2000 Summer Olympic Games in Sydney, Australia—where Wilkinson became one of those stories. With a gold medal draped around her neck as she stood atop the medal stand for the women's 10-meter platform diving competition, Wilkinson symbolized one of the greatest (and most improbable) comeback stories in Olympic history.

More than 40 points behind after the preliminaries, Wilkinson surged from fifth to first on her third of five dives in the final round of competition—a reverse 2 1/2 somersault, which drew four 9.5s from the judges. Then, she locked up the gold by nailing her most difficult dive, an inward 2 1/2 somersault in the pike position, which she had botched in the prelims. Her scores were all 8.5s and 9s. In holding off China's Li Na, Wilkinson captured an event that had not been won by the U.S. in 36 years.

But it was how she won that makes Laura Wilkinson's story so amazing. In March, just five months before the games, she broke the middle three bones in her right foot in a freak training accident: She banged her foot on a piece of plywood used for indoor training while practicing somersaults for the inward 2 1/2.

Still, Wilkinson delayed surgery—knowing the foot would have to be re-broken and set after the Olympics — and pressed on. At times, she wore a T-shirt bearing the message PAIN IS WEAKNESS LEAVING THE BODY. A fused mass of bone on the bottom of her foot made it feel like she constantly walked on a rock. Still, Wilkinson took it one step at a time. She did what she could on crutches for two months. She practiced six hours a day with various types of casts, mounting the platform and visualizing going through her takeoffs and come-outs for every dive on her

Laura Wilkinson receives the gold medal. Shaun Botterill /Allsport/Getty Images

list. When the last of the casts was shed, she still had to wear a protective boot to cushion the climb up the platform—where she had to launch most of her dives from a sitting position. (The first time she attempted to climb the 33-foot tower following the injury, it took her ten minutes to get to the top.) Still, Wilkinson was determined not to let the situation sidetrack her dream. Said her coach Ken Armstrong, "I had never seen that sense of urgency in her [before]."

When Wilkinson reached the top of the platform for her fourth dive of her golden night in Sydney, she knew she was one good dive away from gold. She slowly removed her boot and tossed it down to the pool deck below.

As her name was called, she looked out at those in the stands cheering for her and acknowledged them with a smile, drinking in the moment. She recited a Bible verse to herself, then launched into the same dive that had caused her injury in the first place. Her thoughts at that moment of truth? "It's the same action that I broke my foot on. It makes me nervous as I get close to the platform. Plus, I have to stand on the ball of my foot. But I guess when it got right down to it, it didn't matter anymore. I figured I had nothing to lose."

When it was over, Wilkinson had indeed lost nothing and gained much—including perspective. "I knew that I just wanted to dive because I loved it. I wanted to win a gold medal, but I knew that if I didn't, it wasn't the end of the world. I didn't want to live my life thinking, 'What if?' I guess if you find out that if you want something bad enough, then it means enough to you that fear and pain become unimportant."

Kurt Warner hoists the George Halas Trophy. Jeff Haynes/AFP/Getty Images

KURT WARNER
FROM "WHO IS HE?" TO MVP

In 1999, he was an out-of-nowhere sensation whose story TV commentator Al Michaels dubbed, "Too schmaltzy even for Hollywood." But on the football field, Kurt Warner proved he was the quintessential quarterback—a leader who wanted the ball in his hands when everything was on the line.

In a storybook 1999 season, Warner came from football oblivion into the public consciousness and the football record books, leading the St. Louis Rams to the NFL championship. In the process, he proved that some dreams really do come true. It was the most spectacular and significant rise of any one player during one NFL season.

Warner's odyssey began during the Rams 1999 preseason. The team had signed free-agent quarterback Trent Green away from the Washington Redskins to be their leader in what promised to be a breakthrough season. But in the Rams' penultimate exhibition game, Green went down with a season-ending knee injury, and the team was suddenly placed in Warner's hands.

"We were in shock when Green went down," recalls Rams offensive line coach Jim Hanifan. "We had centered everything on him. He was the quarterback we wanted — and then this, to face the season with a backup."

No one on the Rams coaching staff knew what to expect. Nor did the players, fans, or anyone else. Few people outside of the Rams' organization had even heard of Warner. But by the end of the 1999 season, everyone in the sports world knew this man and his unusual story.

Warner's unlikely path to NFL stardom began in his lone year as a starting quarterback at Division I-AA Northern Iowa, where he sat on the bench for four years. In 1993, when the fifth-year senior finally got his shot, he led the Panthers to the NCAA Division I-AA semifinals and was named first-team all-Gateway Conference, throwing for 2,747 yards and 17 touchdowns.

That performance earned him a free-agent tryout with the Green Bay Packers in 1994. Warner made it to the Packers' camp for the tryout but was cut after running just ten plays in six weeks. With Brett Favre, Mark Brunell, and Ty Detmer in camp, Warner didn't stand a chance of making the Packers' roster. Further, he didn't appear able to lead any team. Once, Steve Marriucci, then the Packers quarterbacks' coach, told him to go into a minicamp scrimmage, but Warner felt so unprepared that he refused.

"There were obviously some good quarterbacks there," recalls Warner. "From a mental standpoint I felt that I had a ways to go—after playing only one year in college — just to get oriented to the system and to be able to pick up the offense. I knew it was going to take me a while within a system and playing more, to really get comfortable with everything that I could do and the speed and quickness of the game. But from a physical standpoint, I felt that I definitely could play."

After being cut by the Packers in the summer of 1994, Warner went home to Cedar Falls, Iowa. He moved in with the parents of then-girlfriend, Brenda Carney, and took a job stocking shelves at a 24-hour supermarket. He continued to prepare for his shot at the NFL, working out and studying football film at his alma mater each day before heading off to work at night. There wasn't much time for sleep.

At the HyVee store where he worked, he happily took home $5.50 an hour while telling coworkers he would someday be playing football again.

"I think inside they were probably thinking *'There's probably no way; I mean, this guy's working in a supermarket — how's he ever going to play in the NFL?'*" recalls Warner. "They listened to me and humored me at the time, but I'm sure, deep down, nobody really expected me to be able to get to the point where I'm at today. I can't blame them. It's a strange story. If I were looking at things from the outside, I would probably have thought the same things they did."

However, out of the blue, the Iowa Barnstormers of the Arena Football League called Warner one day. At first, he wasn't thrilled about the prospect of playing eight-man football, but he figured it was better than nothing. He struggled initially, because he lacked the speed and agility needed for the quick-scoring indoor game. But he adapted and became an Arena League star, passing for 10,164 yards and 183 touchdowns and leading the Barnstormers to two "Arena Bowls" in three seasons.

"Kurt had all the qualities to be a great quarterback," said Barnstormers coach John Gregory. "We knew he had the arm and the intelligence. We just didn't know if he ever would get a chance to show his ability."

Warner had a tryout scheduled with the Chicago Bears in 1997. But it was canceled after the elbow on his throwing arm swelled to the size of a baseball, thanks to a spider bite suffered on his Jamaican honeymoon.

While his quest for big-time pro football seemed at a roadblock, Warner refused to be discouraged. He clung to his dream of playing in the NFL, even when it seemed he didn't have a prayer.

"I've always believed in myself," says Warner. "I always believed that I had the talent to get to this level and to be successful. I was just waiting for the opportunity. I was waiting for that door to open, to get a chance to prove to everybody that I could do it."

Despite his Arena League success, Kurt couldn't get another look from an NFL team. But then Al Luginbill, the coach of NFL Europe's Amsterdam Admirals, came calling. Warner told Luginbill he'd rather keep playing for the

Barnstormers for $65,000 a year than go abroad—unless an NFL team signed him and optioned him to Europe for training. A dozen teams told Luginbill no. Then, finally, Charley Armey, the Rams' personnel director, decided to take a chance.

But then Warner had what he deemed a "horrible" tryout with St. Louis. Fortunately, during that look-see, he gained two key backers: Armey and assistant coach Mike White, who persuaded the team to sign him. Thus in the spring of '98, the Rams sent Warner to Europe to play for Amsterdam.

It was a smart move. Warner led NFL Europe in passing yardage (2,101) and touchdowns (15) and gained a new level of confidence. And his experiences off the field in Amsterdam's open culture solidified the conservative quarterback's character and prepared him to be a leader.

Warner returned to the states in the summer to compete for a spot on the Rams' roster. He earned (barely) the third-string QB job, nearly being released in favor of journeyman Wil Furrer. While the Rams were going 4-12 in '98, Warner saw mop-up action in one game, completing just 4 of 11 passes for 39 yards. His future was still very much in doubt.

In 1999, after being left unprotected by the Rams for the NFL expansion draft, Warner was passed over by the Cleveland Browns, who selected veteran Ty Detmer instead in what would prove to be a glaring error for the Browns, but a boon for the Rams. At the time, however, it was a move few in NFL circles gave any attention.

At the Rams '99 training camp, Warner ended up moving into the Rams' number-two quarterback spot, as Trent Green's understudy. Rams' head coach Dick Vermeil assumed Warner was good enough for the team to get by with, should Green get injured. But he never expected the 28-year-old journeyman to play well enough to be the key reason the Rams won games.

After Green's injury, Warner proceeded to light up the NFL's best defenses. The 6'2", 220-pounder demonstrated impressive arm strength and great touch—and the ability to make all the throws: from laser-like deep outs across the field, to feathery-soft corner lobs, to on-the-money long strikes. He also showed maturity and leadership intangibles, poise under fire, toughness, and an uncanny adeptness for quickly reading defenses—something that takes rookies three to four years to learn. Playing Arena ball, with its small field and wide-open style, had helped Warner become proficient at making quick throws based on even quicker reads.

In the end, 1999 was a year in which Warner generated the second-finest statistical season by a quarterback in NFL history. He completed 65 percent of his passes, threw for 4,353 yards and 41 touchdowns. (In league history, only Dan Marino and Peyton Manning have thrown for more TDs in a single season). His passing rating was the third highest all-time. He led the Rams turnaround from their 4-12 mark in '98 to a 13-3 record and a spot in the Super Bowl and was named the NFL's Player of the Year.

At the Super Bowl, Warner continued his mastery, eclipsing Joe Montana's 11-year-old passing record by throwing for 414 yards. He completed 24 of 45 passes and tossed two touchdowns—including the game winner with a minute and 54 seconds remaining in the contest. He was named the game's Most Valuable Player.

"You know, when you're a little kid, you dream about holding the trophy up after throwing the winning touchdown or scoring the winning touchdown," said Warner. "This is what it's all about. It's what you play for, all those years. To be the starting QB in the Super Bowl, to have won the MVP—you can't ever really think that's going to

Kurt Warner celebrates a 1999 victory over the Cleveland Browns.
Elsa Hasch /Allsport/Getty Images

happen in your first year. But I've always had confidence. I've always felt I could play well."

Warner's story seems almost too good to be true, yet every bit of it is indeed reality. And the person who was most unfazed by it all is the man who lived it. While everyone else may have considered Warner a nobody before the 1999 season, the quarterback inside him saw things quite differently.

"I fell through the cracks just because of the fact that nobody saw me play," notes Warner. "I played only one year in college, and it was at a small school. I played well that one year, but it's hard to put a lot of stock in just one year. It's hard to give a guy that hasn't played very much a great opportunity. I went straight to Arena Football, which we all know nobody really looks at. Finally, I got the opportunity to work out for St. Louis and go to the World League, where I was able to open some eyes—because there were people actually looking at it, and they saw what I could do on a football field. To me, it was more that nobody ever saw me play and could really gauge what kind of quarterback I was, because they weren't looking in the right places."

From anonymous third-stringer to the embodiment of sudden athletic success—all in five months—Kurt Warner is the kind of man that Horatio Alger used to write stories about. In the magical 1999 season, Warner became the consummate symbol of all that is good in sports.

"Kurt Warner is Kurt Warner," Coach Vermeil said following the Super Bowl triumph. "He is not a fairy tale. This is real life. He is an example of what we all like to believe in, on and off the field. He is an example of persistence and believing in himself. What else can you write? He is a book, he is a movie, the guy."

"I've learned a lot along the way," Warner says. "I've learned about perseverance. I've learned about being humble, being able to enjoy everything that I've gotten. I wouldn't change anything from the way it has turned out. I've become a better player and a better person throughout the experiences I've had. I wouldn't change anything. This is as good a script as I could have ever written."

Derek Redmond at the Olympic Trials in Birmingham, England, 1988
Bob Martin/Allsport/Getty Images

DEREK REDMOND
A GOLDEN MOMENT

The 1992 Summer Olympic Games were destined to become one of the most touching and memorable in history. In Barcelona, Spain, emotion was high as much of the world had just come through the tension of the Gulf War. The Olympics provided an opportunity to rebuild a sense of peace and goodwill among nations. No event from the '92 games made a greater impact on the world in creating a lasting image of unity than a 400 meter semifinal race in track and field.

British track star Derek Redmond was a favorite

to be among those on the medal podium at the end of competition. He had his heart set on winning gold. Yet what happened to Redmond would not result in a gold medal, but rather a golden moment.

In the middle of the race, Redmond seemed to be running smoothly and preparing for a strong finish that would earn him a preferred lane in the finals. Then, suddenly, he stopped, grabbed the back of his leg, and fell to the track in a crumpled heap. The dream was over. Redmond's pursuit of Olympic glory had come to a crushing halt.

Still, the runner was not to be defeated. With his face showing the excruciating pain caused from what he would later learn was a torn hamstring, Redmond was determined to finish the race. He rose from the track, his competitors now a hundred yards ahead, and began to hobble toward the finish line. Each step was marked by agony. The crowd gasped collectively, as if they could feel the pain Redmond was experiencing. His will was strong, but it appeared his leg would not hold out. Still, like a wounded animal, he attempted to continue.

Within moments, Redmond's father, Jim, jumped out

Derek Redmond is comforted by his father after suffering an injury during the 400 meter semifinal in Barcelona. STAFF/AFP/Getty Images

of the stands and made his way toward the track. When security personnel attempted to stop him, Jim Redmond yelled, "That's my son!" He was admitted onto the track, where he came to Derek's aid.

When he reached his son's side, Jim grabbed his arm and said, "You don't have to do this."

"Yes I do," Derek responded.

With that, Jim draped Derek's left arm around his own shoulders. Next, he placed his right arm around his son's shoulders. Then he grabbed Derek's right arm and began to lead him to the finish line. With his father walking beside him, Derek hopped along gingerly and completed the last portion of the race. Together, slowly, father and son made it down the front stretch and reached the finish line while an amazed crowd rose to their feet and roared with wild cheers. The image was captured by photographers and television cameras and was quickly beamed around the world in what has become one of the most emotional and inspiring moments in Olympic history.

The official results of the men's 400-meter semifinal race show Derek Redmond's performance as "race abandoned." The world will remember it as anything but.

Indeed, this race will long be remembered as a moment as unifying as track and field has ever seen—when a father and son came together to finish the race, in one of the most remarkable displays of compassion and teamwork in sports history.

Kerri Strug carries the Olympic Flame. Todd Warshaw/Pool/Getty Images

KERRI STRUG

A COURAGEOUS SACRIFICE

K erri Strug was the last hope Team USA had for gold in the 1996 Olympic women's team gymnastics competition in Atlanta. To help the U.S. team defeat the dominant Russians, Strug would have to deliver on the vault.

Her first attempt was not good enough. She was a bit off balance leaving the springboard, and she couldn't quite get her body straightened out in the air. The minuscule error in balance resulted in an awkward landing. Her left ankle took the brunt of the impact with the mat. Strug heard a cracking noise, then felt excruciating pain. She knew something was wrong but tried to walk it off. She glanced at the scoreboard. The judges' marks were not enough to push the Americans ahead of the Russians.

So, the gymnast faced a decision. She could sit out the next jump and get herself ready for the individual all-around event that would take place the following week—and forfeit her team's chance for gold in the vault competition. Or, she could put pain aside and try one more vault, risking severe injury and jeopardizing her shot at individual gold.

Kerri Strug had precious few seconds to decide. With the crowd roaring wildly for her and her ankle throbbing, she made up her mind.

She decided to go for it. Placing her individual opportunity for glory aside, she said a prayer and ran fearlessly toward the vault. She hit the springboard perfectly, thrust herself off the apparatus and into the air . . . and nailed the landing—practically on one leg.

Strug collapsed in pain as her teammates and coaches rushed toward her. As the tears flooded down her cheeks, coach Bela Karolyi picked her up and carried her to the team seating area.

The mark came up. A 9.90 flashed on the scoreboard,

meaning Team USA had won the gold medal in the women's team gymnastics competition—for the first time in Olympic history.

Afterward, U.S. team doctors informed Kerri that she had sustained two torn ligaments in her ankle, thus eliminating herself from the individual competition. Now she had no chance of achieving an individual gold medal, a dream she had worked at for nearly 15 years.

A coach found her crying over the missed opportunity to compete in the all-around championships and encouraged her by saying, "Kerri, sometimes you don't reach all your goals in life."

But clearly, Kerri Strug had reached one major goal. In sacrificing her personal dreams for the benefit of the team, she made history by becoming the star of the first-ever American women's gold-medal gymnastics team. And she became a true Olympic hero in the process.

David Robinson celebrates victory at the 2003 NBA finals. Matt Rourke/AFP/Getty Images

DAVID ROBINSON
AN ADMIRAL ON LAND AND SEA

I t was a classic example of David versus Goliath. In this case, the David was surnamed Robinson, the magnificent 7-1 center for the San Antonio Spurs. The Goliath was the huge tower of expectations he faced ever since he came into the NBA in 1989. No matter what Robinson accomplished over his first nine years in the league, his "Goliath" would not go away. What Robinson needed to vanquish the expectations, it seemed, were five smooth stones and a slingshot.

Robinson's NBA career had begun well. In fact, he had

been nothing short of phenomenal. In his first season, he was named NBA Rookie of the Year, and he led the Spurs to one of the biggest single-year turnarounds in pro basketball history. Without him, in the 1988-89 season, the Spurs went 21-61. The following season, Robinson's first, they improved to 56-26, won the Midwest Division, and immediately became a title contender and one of the most feared teams in the NBA.

Robinson continued to improve. He led the league in rebounds in 1991 and in blocked shots in '92—the same year he was named the NBA's Defensive Player of the Year. He won the scoring championship in 1994. He was selected as the league's MVP in '95. In 1996, as part of the NBA's 50th-anniversary celebration, Robinson was named one of the 50 greatest players in league history.

Further, he became a fixture on U.S. Olympic teams, representing the United States in 1988 (Seoul, South Korea), 1992 (Barcelona, Spain), and 1996 (Atlanta, Georgia). He was the first male to be selected to three Olympic basketball teams and became the leading scorer and rebounder in U.S. Olympic history.

Meanwhile, back in San Antonio, Robinson's Spurs

won an average of 55 games over his first seven seasons—capturing the division title four times. But until 1999, there was still one thing Robinson had not accomplished—the famous gaping hole in his basketball resume. In all his NBA seasons, David Robinson had not won an NBA championship, and the critics wanted to know why.

Some in the media questioned Robinson's heart—his resolve and toughness. They were quick to label him "soft," acknowledging that he was a fine player but suggesting that he wasn't tough enough to win a world championship. They compared him, unfavorably, with greats like Jabbar, Russell, Chamberlain, Malone, Olajuwon, West, Bird, Magic, and Jordan—all of whom led their teams to NBA titles.

What the media conveniently failed to remember, however, was that Chamberlain and West had each other, along with Elgin Baylor. Jabbar and Magic also played together—and also had tough supporting players like James Worthy on their side. Russell had Bob Cousy. Malone had Ralph Sampson. Olajuwon had a bevy of great outside shooters. Bird had Kevin McHale and Robert Parrish. Jordan had Scottie Pippen.

Robinson, meanwhile, had a supporting cast featuring

the likes of Greg Anderson and Vinny Del Negro. Decent players but nowhere near the caliber of the McHales and Pippens of the NBA world.

Certainly, the Spurs did have a few of the pieces needed to build a championship team. There was underrated point guard Avery Johnson, Robinson's best friend on the team. And Sean Elliott, who could be counted on to knock down key shots. What was missing was another dominant offensive and defensive force, someone who could share the scoring and rebounding load with Robinson.

Then came 1997. That year, the Spurs won the NBA draft lottery and found the missing piece to their championship puzzle. With the first selection in the '97 draft, San Antonio picked Collegiate Player of the Year Tim Duncan, whom many consider the most complete player in the pro game.

The 7-foot Duncan gave the Spurs "twin towers"— and the opposition twin headaches. In Duncan, Robinson had a teammate who gave opponents fits on offense and defense. No longer could Houston, L.A., Utah, or Portland merely double-team Robinson in the playoffs and leave it to a role player to save the game for San Antonio.

Now Robinson had his sidekick, his fellow giant-slay-

er. Robinson was so grateful for the help that he was willing to let Duncan take center stage. He let Duncan become the Spurs go-to-guy. The rookie was the team's Jordan or Bird, while Robinson willingly played the role of Pippen or McHale. The Spurs' megastar gave up the "mega." He relinquished the glamour, the shots, and the celebrity for the good of the team. He played defense, blocked shots, battled toe-to-toe with the league's bullies, and did the rebounding grunt-work on the offensive boards. Not only did he do it —and do it well—he did it without complaining

Just two years previously, Robinson had signed the richest contract in pro sports history. Now he was playing second fiddle. It was like Pavarotti singing second tenor. Hemingway ghostwriting a first-timer's novel. Bogart getting second billing. It was one of the most remarkable things ever seen in sport. And it paid off.

In 1999, Duncan's second year with the team, the Spurs, centering their offense on a second-year player, brought the NBA title to the city of the Alamo, defeating the New York Knicks in the finals.

And with that, David's "Goliath" was finally vanquished. And it happened because Robinson had become a "David" in every sense of the word. He let another star shine more brightly.

"How many superstars would've done it?" said Spurs coach Gregg Popovich, reflecting on Robinson's sacrifice. "Not many."

"In today's NBA?" echoed teammate Sean Elliott. "I'd say none."

"I guess I just figured winning was more important than anything else I could do for the team," Robinson explained.

Robinson's approach is exactly what one would hope to see from a true sportsman, which Robinson clearly is. He plunged into a two-year process of self-denial that put the Spurs in position to win the coveted NBA title.

Robinson devoted himself, on and off the court, to mentoring Duncan and making him the best possible player. He was determined to adapt his game to fit Duncan's. In effect, Robinson became Duncan's understudy, supporting him in his starring role—and taking center stage only in those rare occasions when Duncan was in foul trouble or battling injuries.

The Spurs' go-to guy became the go-from guy.

"It wasn't a painless thing," Elliott noted. "David had to make some adjustments. But near the end of the season, I saw it coming together."

And what about those charges that Robinson was too soft to win the big games?

"You don't win a rebounding title or a defensive player of the year award in this league and be soft," says Popovich.

The problem for Robinson was that he was such a graceful athlete that even when he was working hard, he appeared placid. He exhibited self-control on and off the court. That, and the fact that he is a man of character made him misunderstood.

But soft?

When he entered the NBA, Robinson was rumored to be the next Bill Russell—with a better shot. In many ways, Robinson lived up to the billing. He was a great defensive player and phenomenal shot blocker who, up until '99, had been asked to carry the load offensively as well. Perhaps no player in NBA history had ever been asked to carry as much of a burden for his team.

Robinson didn't demand a huge contract for his huge efforts. He could have started a bidding war for his talents when his contract ended after the '96-97 season. Many teams showed interest in him, including the Spurs' arch-rival, the big-spending Los Angeles Lakers. Instead, well before his contract deadline, Robinson re-signed with the Spurs for well under his market value. His modest contract enabled the Spurs to preserve enough salary-cap room to sign Duncan when he became available in the draft.

It's hard to imagine another star player not only less infatuated with himself than Robinson, but also less in love with his money.

For example, in 1997, Robinson and his wife, Valerie, announced a $5 million gift to establish The Carver Academy at San Antonio's Carver Center, a multicultural and multiethnic community center.

"We've tried to meet people's needs in San Antonio on a basic level," Robinson explains. "But we wanted to do more. The Carver has had a great impact on this community for 100 years. And it is a big part of the black community, which means a lot to us. I have a heart that wants to serve and bless. That is what I am."

But it's not necessarily what Robinson has always been. In fact, Robinson really never even thought about a

Robinson goes for two against the Suns in 2000. © Reuters/CORBIS

career in basketball until he was nearly finished at the U.S. Naval Academy. He grew up playing classical piano and jazz saxophone instead of pick-up basketball games at the neighborhood court. As an elementary school student, he was enrolled in programs for gifted students. In junior high, he took college-level computer classes and built his own big-screen TV from a kit. Baseball was his favorite sport, although he played most others, except basketball. His first experience on a basketball team came during his senior year in high school.

Then, after scoring a blistering 1,320 on the SAT college entrance exam (out of a possible 1,600), Robinson went to Navy as a 6-6, 175-pound future sailor studying engineering and mathematics.

As a freshman at Navy, he averaged 7 points and 4 rebounds per game and seemed uncomfortable on the court—and only marginally interested in the game. But over the next four years, he grew seven inches, and basketball seemed to be made for him.

As a senior, Robinson emerged as the nation's top college player, then became the first pick in the '87 draft. After graduating with a degree in mathematics, he fulfilled

his two-year service commitment to the Navy prior to joining the Spurs.

From the day Robinson was drafted, fans and media in San Antonio expected an NBA championship from their superstar. He eventually delivered—but in an unconventional way. In the process, he demonstrated what great athletes are really all about: the team.

An exultant Cynthia Cooper displays the WNBA championship trophy in Houston, 2000. Ronald Martinez /Allsport/Getty Images

CYNTHIA COOPER
FINDING TRIUMPH AMID TRAGEDY

As the first-ever star of women's professional basketball in America, Cynthia Cooper was an anomaly. She was gracious and austere off the court, but intense and driven when playing. At 37, she would seem to have been an athlete past her prime, yet at that age she finished her career in 2000 maintaining her role as the most dominant player in the WNBA and leading her team to an unprecedented fourth consecutive championship.

Cooper was the league's first superstar and MVP during each of its first two seasons. She led the Houston Comets to the league title in each of the league's first four years of existence, 1997-2000. And when she retired following the 2000 season, she did so fulfilled in knowing she was the one person most responsible for giving the fledgling league a solid identity right from the get-go.

But while Cooper was dazzling fans on the court night in and night out, her insides were churning as she walked through intense personal tragedy. Her smile and pleasant nature belied the burdens she carried while lifting her sport to professional acceptance.

Those close to her know, however, what Cooper has had to endure. They saw it when she affixed a pink ribbon to her uniform to signify her support for breast-cancer research. They saw it when she used to hurry into the Houston locker room after each road game to call her mother, Mary Cobbs, who eventually died from the disease in 1999. They saw it when Comets' coach Van Chancellor moved practice back by a half an hour once in a while so Cooper had time to take her mom for another battery of tests or a chemotherapy treatment session. They saw it when Cooper wistfully looked at photos or the jersey of former teammate, roommate, and close-friend Kim Perrot, who died of cancer in 1999.

After all, it was Perrot herself who used to stay up

late at night with Cooper when the team was on the road, talking about holding onto hope and why bad things happened to good people.

Being on the court seemed to be a relief for Cooper. She was a pure scorer who exuded an "I dare you to stop me" attitude. The league's all-time scoring leader, she was equally as comfortable draining a jumper in a defender's face as she was whisking by her on the way to the hoop.

While she was vivacious on the court, Cooper tends to be stoic about herself and her off-the-court challenges. She will not easily volunteer information regarding the emotions she has struggled with or how she came to the aid of both her mother and Perrot. Few know, for example, that Cynthia escorted her mom through every stage of her cancer treatment in '97. Or that she frequently stayed up until 3 a.m. to do the ironing and other household chores for her mother. Neither do many know that she has helped raise a niece and nephew, and has adopted another nephew, Tyquon. All together, she now has five nieces and nephews who live with her.

For Cooper, playing through a hamstring pull or ankle sprain was minimal in comparison to what her mother endured or what Perrot went through.

Cynthia Cooper intent on a jump shot   Bill Baptist/WNBAE/Getty Images

Mary Cobbs learned she had breast cancer just weeks after she and her daughter received the joyful news that the WNBA had assigned Cooper to play in Houston, the family's adopted home town. At least there, Cooper thought, she would be home enough to help care for her mother.

"It was unbelievable how it all worked out," Cooper says.

While the WNBA was marketed as the game that would be ruled by such media darlings as Lisa Leslie and Rebecca Lobo, it was Cooper who took the league by storm. The 5'10" shooting guard displayed her all-around game and for four years outplayed the others, quickly setting the league's single-game scoring record with 44 points only 10 games into the season.

"She's the best all-around player I've ever faced," said New York Liberty guard Vickie Johnson.

Her success in the WNBA was a far cry from the tears she shed as a youngster. Cooper spent her teenage years in a crime-ridden neighborhood in the Watts section of Los Angeles. Her mother made significant sacrifices to raise Cynthia and her seven siblings. Sports became a way out of the pain of a childhood partially lost. Even then, Cooper's basketball career didn't begin until she was 16, and then it was only accidental.

"I just happened to be in the gym at my junior high school one day and saw this older girl come down the court, put the ball behind her back from her left to her right hand, and then make a lay-up," Cooper recalls. "Up until then I had run track. But just like that I said, 'Oooh. Wow. I want to play like that someday.'"

By her senior year in high school, Cooper was good enough to be recruited by colleges in the West. She chose the University of Southern California, where she played a supporting role on the 1983 and '84 teams that won NCAA championships and featured Cheryl Miller and the McGee Twins, Pam and Paula. She also played on two U.S. Olympic teams, earning a gold medal at the '88 games in Seoul, South Korea, and a bronze at Barcelona in '92. But through all that, Cooper says she never felt completely challenged to utilize all of her talents.

"I never felt like I had given all I was capable of giving to one of my teams," she explains. "I was always the sort of player who was asked to pass the ball to the marquee players and set picks, run the fast break. My role might be to come into the game to be a defensive stopper or a spark plug. But all along, I told myself, 'This is not my game. This is not who I am as a basketball player. And this is not all I can do.'"

The evolution of her game began during her 11 seasons as a pro in Europe, beginning in 1986.

She became that superstar type of player with the teams Alcamo and Parma in the Italian league. In the 1995-96 season, Cooper averaged 35.5 points per game for Alcamo. She arrived in the WNBA as a full-fledged, known scorer. To become such, her work regimen at times included firing up 300-500 shots per day in practice. And it all paid off.

In the first WNBA season, Cooper led the league in scoring at 22.2 per game and was also selected as the title game MVP after a 25-point effort. She began to receive endorsement offers and show up on talk shows and in WNBA promotional spots. She was now the league's true marquee player, much like those she had grown accustomed to playing caddie to years before.

In the aftermath of that first, glorious season, Cooper would say it was all the more sweet for her in that she was able to share it with her mother.

"I've been tucked away in Europe for 11 years, and my mom hasn't been able to share any of the special moments," she said at the time. "She's my MVP."

In '98, she repeated her performance in a nearly

identical fashion, scoring 22.7 points per game to lead the league—and again leading her team to the title and a 27-3 regular season record.

But 1999 would provide the biggest challenge yet. There were the expectations to win a third consecutive title, but other burdens grew even heavier.

Cooper turned in her third straight outstanding performance on the court—and in the finals—and again led the league in scoring at 22.1 points per game while also leading in assists at 5.7 per game. But in the midst of her continuing excellence, she faced her most difficult defeats.

On February 12, 1999, Cooper's mother lost her battle with breast cancer. Ten days later, Perrot was diagnosed with lung cancer that had spread to her brain. In six months, Cooper's close friend was dead at the age of 32. Following the '99 finals win, Cooper stood atop the media table near centercourt and held aloft Perrot's jersey as if to tell the world she and her teammates had won it all for their fallen friend. It was a victory she seemed to will herself and her team to.

"There isn't but one Cynthia Cooper," asserts Chancellor. "She's got the greatest will to win of any player I've ever seen, man or woman. I've heard a lot about Larry

[Bird], Magic [Johnson] and Michael [Jordan] having the greatest will to win, but I'm going to put Cynthia Cooper up there against anybody."

"I don't know if there is another person on the planet who could have handled it the way she handled it," says Cooper's 2000 U.S. Olympic team coach, Nell Fortner. "Triumphed with the memory of her mother and Kim Perrot in the forefront and leading Houston to the finals at the top of her game. She's got an inner strength that I don't know if anybody can match."

Cooper finished her wondrous basketball tour with a fourth straight WBNA title and fourth straight finals MVP award in 2000. Then she simply walked away from the game the same way she first entered—with grace, class, and composure, and as a model of how to prioritize one's life.

The intensity of Dave Johnson   Tony Duffy /Allsport/Getty Images

DAVE JOHNSON
THE METTLE TO MEDAL

For months, leading up to the 1992 Summer Olympic Games in Barcelona, Spain, the "Dan & Dave" promotional campaign told the world about the coming duel between Dan O'Brien and Dave Johnson for the title of "world's greatest athlete" and the gold medal in the decathlon competition. While neither would ultimately claim gold, it was Dave who grabbed the hearts of the nation with one of the most stirring and courageous performances in Olympic history.

Johnson won the bronze medal in Barcelona with a score of 8,309 points. The total was far below his U.S.

Olympic Trials-winning total of 8,649, but an astonishing performance considering the courage it took to compete with a stress fracture in his right ankle—an injury he sustained just weeks before the games. How could he hurdle on a bone that could crack open on any landing? "It hurts so much I can't even feel it," Johnson would finally reveal moments after his Olympic ordeal was over.

Johnson was no stranger to trial by the time he hit Barcelona. He had persevered through numerous injuries and surgeries, as well as the sorrow he endured when he and wife, Sherrie, lost their first baby to miscarriage. Still, Johnson never complained during the competition and hasn't complained in the years that have followed.

"The Olympics taught me a very valuable lesson about setting goals, one that any athlete can apply to his own experience," says Johnson. "My goal in Barcelona was to win the gold medal. Pure and simple. But how could I account for the stress fracture? I had never felt pain like that before. It was as if knives were sticking into my foot and shooting out through the other side.

"I heard a pop during the 110-meter hurdles, and that's when the bone in my foot splintered into two distinct pieces," Johnson explains. "The swelling increased so much

that I couldn't even fit into my shoe for the pole vault. Now what was I going to do? Quitting wasn't an option. I didn't even want anyone to know about the fracture. But I had to face facts. The goal had shifted from winning to finishing. I told myself to just suck it up and run on pain and faith.

The record book will forever show that Johnson placed third in the event he was favored to win, 312 points behind gold medalist Robert Zmelik of Czechoslovakia. Yet he finished first in another race—this one against near-impossible odds.

Said amazed teammate Rob Muzzio when asked to assess the performance of his U.S. teammate, "There was so much pressure put on him. Considering the injury…he did awesome… His 1,500, he was in so much pain. The guy's got guts."

While his medal is bronze, Dave Johnson's effort and demonstration of physical discipline will remain forever golden.

"Never allow a preconceived goal to interfere with your ability to adapt and improvise," Johnson says. "I can live with the bronze medal. I learned so much from getting that bronze, I'm not sure a gold would have taught me as much."

Jackie Robinson played for the Brooklyn Dodgers from 1947-1956
National Baseball Hall of Fame Library/MLB Photos/Getty Images

JACKIE ROBINSON
THE COLOR OF COURAGE

O n April 15, 1947, Jackie Robinson crossed the white line. He crossed the white chalk line that outlined the baseball diamond and the line of color separation that kept America's game in bondage to bigotry. But Robinson didn't just break baseball's color barrier by becoming the first black major leaguer of the century. He also set into motion the most sweeping social changes in the nation's history. For the first time, America had a black hero at the very center of the its consciousness. More than his talent, it was Robinson's resolve and extraordinary self-control that made it possible.

Brooklyn Dodgers president Branch Rickey signed Robinson with the intent of seeing him as the torch-bearer for integration in baseball. Rickey prepared his young athlete for the barrage he would have to endure in '47, knowing the first black player would have to survive all manner of provocation—emotional and physical. In Robinson, he saw a man with the fortitude to withstand even the harshest of opposition.

Robinson endured the most vicious treatment any athlete has ever faced. He was the target of racial epithets and flying cleats, of hate letters and death threats, of pitchers throwing at his head and legs, and catchers spitting on his shoes. In the midst of this chaos, there was a circus-like quality to Dodgers games, with Robinson on display. Large crowds, including many African-Americans, cheered his pop-ups and ground-outs. The daily papers singled him out by use of racial monikers rather than by name. "More eyes were on Jackie than on any rookie who ever played," recalls Rex Barney, a Brooklyn reliever that year.

As the first days unfolded, the pressure increased. Police investigated letters that had threatened Robinson's life. "He turned them over to me," announced Rickey. "Two of the notes were so vicious that I felt they should be

investigated." The pressure also involved Robinson's lodging when the Dodgers arrived in Philly. The players usually stayed at the Benjamin Franklin Hotel, but when they arrived there, the hotel manager turned them away, telling the team's traveling secretary, Harold Parrott, "Don't bring your team back here while you have any Nigras with you!" The Dodgers ended up staying at the Warrick. Parrott later wrote that Robinson looked pained over the incident, "knowing we were pariahs because of him." In the midst of such turmoil, Robinson soldiered on. "I'm just going along playing the best ball I know and doing my best to make good," he said. "Boy, it's rugged."

Robinson eventually won over most observers. He was named National League Rookie of the Year in 1947 and went on to be voted the league's Most Valuable Player two years later. During his ten seasons, the Dodgers won six pennants and a world championship. He was the team's catalyst, a second baseman who found numerous ways to beat the opponent. He was daring and exuded a competitive fire. He won a batting title, drove in 100 runs in a season, stole home 19 times, and hardly ever struck out.

Robinson's middle infield partner, shortstop Harold "Pee Wee" Reese, remembering his friend's display of

The September 22, 1947, cover of TIME

courage, said, "I don't know any other ballplayer who could have done what he did—to be able to hit with everybody yelling at him. He had to block all that out. To do what he did has got to be the most tremendous thing I've ever seen in all of sports."

"I'm not concerned with you liking or disliking me," Robinson said. "All I ask is that you respect me as a human being."

Respect came from the entire nation, as did admiration. Robinson had not only carried the future of the game on his back, but also the future of an entire people. The sense of burden was not lost on him, yet he never showed it publicly, choosing instead to constantly demonstrate self-control. In so doing, he gave to baseball and his country more than he had ever dreamed possible.

Jim Ryun in the 1500 meters, Munich, 1972   John Dominis//Time Life Pictures/Getty Images

JIM RYUN
FINDING BALANCE

The year was 1964. The feat was one of the more incredible accomplishments in all of sports. The person who achieved the milestone was a skinny teenager from rural Kansas who no one had ever heard of before. But he set the track world on its proverbial ear.

More than 35 years ago, then-17-year-old Jim Ryun ran the first-ever sub-four-minute high school mile. What made the record all the more amazing is that Ryun, now a Republican congressman in Kansas, is almost 50 percent deaf. Along with lifelong inner ear damage came equilibrium problems. Ryun is perhaps the only person ever to have less trouble setting world records than staying on his feet.

Ryun never could hear the cleats of approaching runners crunching behind him. Videotapes confirm as much, showing the quick peeks he took at those trailing while winning races like the 1967 AAU National Championships mile.

"Sometimes it was mistaken as taunting my competitors," explained Ryun, who that year set a world record of 3 minutes, 51.5 seconds. The record stood for nine years.

But Ryun's suffering was not confined to his ears. His equilibrium problems also led to a number of near-falls on the track.

He recalls flirting with such a mishap when he ran a 3.59 mile in 1964 while a junior at Wichita Kansas East High School.

"About a lap and a half into it, I'm bumped by another runner, and I actually stepped into the infield of the track," says Ryun, whose 3.53.3 in '65 remains the U.S. prep record.

"I'm on my feet, so I got back into the race. What I said during that time is, I'm much like a guy on stilts. I tip over very easily.

"When I'm in a crowd, I have a tendency to run with

Jim Ryun in a pre-Olympic race, 1972   Tony Duffy /Allsport/Getty Images

my elbows a little wide and put my feet a little wider because I do fall easily."

During his freshman year at Kansas, Ryun underwent tests at the university medical center to see if his equilibrium could be improved. It could not. So he learned to live with it, as well as the consequences.

Those included his share of disappointments on the track as well, including perhaps one of the sport's most infamous falls.

In a 1,500 meter qualifying heat at the 1972 Olympics in Munich, Germany, Ryun was bumped from behind, stumbled, fell to the track, and was eliminated. Just like that, the gold that was all but assured him by expert predictions was gone. Ryun never did run to Olympic stardom as was projected for him, showing the nature of competition, timing, and being a marked man.

In 1968, just as he was gearing up for the Mexico City Olympic games, Ryun came down with mononucleosis, which cut the heart out of his training. Nonetheless, he went to the games in sub-par physical condition as the prohibitive favorite to win the gold.

Racing in Mexico City's 7,000-foot-plus elevation, flatlander Ryun was at a disadvantage against Kenyan Kip

Keino. He finished second in what is still considered a stunning upset. Years later, Ben Jipsho, Keino's Kenyan teammate, admitted that he and Keino had conspired to bring Ryun down. Jipcho took the race out fast, hoping to drain Ryun and take away his kick.

"Everyone goes through stumbles at some point in their lives," Ryun says philosophically, "It's a matter of getting up and being willing to go on."

Michelle Akers in 1999 before a game against the FIFA Allstars
Aubrey Washington /Allsport/Getty Images

MICHELLE AKERS
PLAYING HURT

The road to athletic glory is littered with tales of tragedy. Obstacles often become large enough to derail many a dream. The best athletes have learned how to turn their challenges into opportunities.

Michelle Akers' story is not unlike many world-class athletes. She started at the bottom and worked hard to make it to the top. In between, there have been a number of ups and downs—struggles that helped define her career and mold her character.

But the difference for Akers, the U.S. women's soccer star, is that her highs have been like Mount Everest, while her lows have been like Death Valley.

A member of the original U.S. women's national team, Akers was the world's first soccer superstar. Fifteen years later, she had an Olympic gold medal and a World Cup championship along with hundreds of individual honors. At the highest of highs, she's been the captain of the greatest team in the world, called the world's greatest player—the Michael Jordan or Wayne Gretzky of women's soccer.

But she also has suffered through a painful divorce, numerous sport related-injuries, including 13 knee surgeries, and a debilitating bout with Chronic Fatigue Syndrome. At the lowest of lows, she's been nearly suicidal.

The desire to be the best is what initially drove Akers in her childhood. It's what also would nearly drive her to destruction.

Raised in Seattle, she dreamed of playing wide receiver for the Pittsburgh Steelers, practicing 'Hail Mary' catches with her brother in the family's back yard until a teacher told her girls don't play football. After getting over that disappointment, Akers attacked other sports with gusto. She became a standout in soccer, basketball, and softball for four years at Shorecrest High School, earning three-time All-American status. From there, she went on to Central

Florida University, where she earned All-American honors all four years and won the inaugural Hermann Award—women's collegiate soccer's version of the Heisman Trophy—in 1988. She graduated as the school's all-time leader in scoring and assists and had her uniform number retired.

She joined the U.S. Women's National Team in 1985 during her freshman year at UCF and scored the first goal in National Team history. In '89, she became a full-time member of the team, as she was first gaining recognition as the best player in the world.

She remembers those early years when players received $10 a day in meal money and had to carry their own bags.

Back then, the Americans were overmatched by teams from countries where soccer is an integral part of the culture. The Europeans elbowed the U.S. players, pulled their shirts, spat at them, and beat them. But the U.S. team learned fast, with the determined Akers leading the way.

When Akers flew back from the inaugural Women's World Cup, held in China in 1991, an elderly lady sitting next to her on the plane asked where Michelle had been. She explained that she had just played in the world championship soccer tournament.

"How'd you do?" the woman asked.

"We won," said Akers.

"That's nice," the woman said.

The win was more than just nice. The 2-1 win over Norway in the final gave U.S. soccer its first world championship since 1962. But the brief interchange showed Akers how much farther she needed to go to bring the team and the sport into the American mainstream.

With each challenge, Akers went into attack mode. Relentless in her preparation and her play on the field, she quickly became acknowledged by all as the world's premier player following the '91 World Cup. She scored an unheard of 10 goals in five games, leading team USA to the championship, and was selected as the tournament Most Valuable Player. Later that year, she was named the FIFA World Cup Golden Boot Winner and the U.S. Olympic Committee Athlete of the Year. She was quite literally on top of the world. But to get there Akers had consistently run on full throttle, using all cylinders. Burnout was lurking, and she had nowhere to go but down.

From such tall heights, falls can be devastating. And they were for Akers.

In the aftermath of World Cup glory, she struggled for two

years with unexplained fatigue and injuries, eventually collapsing on the field at the Olympic Sports Festival. She was diagnosed with Chronic Fatigue Immune Dysfunction Syndrome (CFIDS), a disease that saps strength and energy to the point that it makes it hard to get through a normal daily routine, much less compete as an athlete at the world-class level.

She ended up testifying before Congress in 1996 at a hearing on CFIDS:

Michelle Akers in action, Women's World Cup quarterfinal, USA v. Germany, 1999
Tim Sloan/AFP/Getty Images

"On the very bad day, it is all I can do to survive," Akers said in her testimony at the hearing. "I walk off— drag myself off the field, my legs and body like lead... My breathing is labored. It is all I can do to get to the locker room, change my clothes, and keep from crying from utter exhaustion. I am light-headed and shaky. My vision is blurred. My teammates ask me if I am okay, and I nod, yes. But my eyes tell the truth. They are hollow, empty.

"I slowly get to my truck and concentrate on the road, willing myself to keep moving, not to pull over and rest. 'Almost there,' I tell myself. 'Just a few more minutes.' By the time I arrive home, I leave my bags in a pile by the door and collapse on the couch. I have no energy to eat, to shower, to call someone for help.

"When it was bad, I couldn't sit up in a chair. All I could do was lie in bed. At night I sweated so much that I went through two or three T-shirts. And the migraine headaches pounded. Boom! Boom! Boom!

"You don't sleep, your balance and short-term memory are gone; I've gotten lost going to the grocery store."

Her battle with CFIDS brought Akers' world crashing down.

"I was so sick that I couldn't take a five-minute walk

without needing two days on the couch to recover," she recalls. "I was forced to spend a lot of time thinking about who I was. That was the hardest thing. It scared me to death."

But Akers overcame her disease just as she had done in adversity so many times before. Many times teammates had seen her indomitable spirit in the face of injury. Along with her 13 knee surgeries, she has suffered many physical setbacks that may have knocked out lesser competitors.

In 1999, she had her face shattered in a collision during a match against the World All Stars. Akers went up to head a ball, and her face met with the back of another player's head, causing three fractures around her eye and face, a concussion, and the need for 25 stitches—and left her looking as if she had just stepped out of the ring with Evander Holyfield. Her left eye was swollen shut for more than a week. But in her ever-determined style, Akers was back on the field in four weeks—and just four days after reconstructive surgery on her cheekbone—in preparation for the 1999 World Cup.

Akers was once the leading scorer in the world—since surpassed by teammate Mia Hamm. During her 1992 season in Sweden, she scored 43 goals in only 24 games, more than any other player—male or female—in the country. As

U.S. coach Tony DiCicco explains, "She was Mia before there was Mia."

Her intense desire allowed Akers to share the podium at the four biggest competitions of her life, raising the cup at the World Cup finals in 1991, '95, and '99; and wearing Olympic gold around her neck in Atlanta in 1996. In 1998, Michelle was presented with the FIFA Order of Merit—the organization's highest honor—given previously only to Henry Kissinger and Nelson Mandela. She was also selected that year as the CONCACAF (Confederation of North, Central American and Caribbean Association Football) Top Woman Player of the 20th Century.

No soccer fan will ever forget Michelle Akers' most amazing moment—her courageous performance in the '99 World Cup final against China. Just six days after America celebrated its independence, Michelle and her teammates hoisted the World Cup with a dramatic shoot-out triumph. But it was not without an intense struggle for their veteran leader.

"After some games, I am so completely undone because of Chronic Fatigue and Immune Dysfunction Syndrome and its resulting repercussions on my body, that I am unable to function for days," she explains. "I knew that to play my game would take everything I had and more,

and unfortunately I knew the consequences well.

"I walked out on to that field with my teammates and before 90,185 of our closest friends knowing I might get pummeled, take a hit in the head, or have to endure 90 minutes of soccer while I was sick as a dog. It isn't anything heroic or mind-boggling. It is simply exacting preparation, a steadfast faith, and an unswerving commitment to run my race so I can cross my finish line with the pride and satisfaction of knowing I gave my all."

Before the final game, Akers, who was staying in a single room due to her CFIDS difficulties, spent her time alone writing in her journal. Before leaving her room for the Rose Bowl she wrote, "Who will I be when I return to this room after the game and look into the mirror? I don't know. I think the key is I'm willing to put myself on the line to find out."

Her role in the very physical final was to keep China's top scorer from shooting, to control the midfield area, to direct the team on the field, and to control and distribute the ball to her teammates. She gave everything she had until she had no more to give. For the entire second half, Akers was delirious.

"With about 15 minutes left in regulation time, I started getting a little loopy," she recounts. "The 110-degree heat on the field, combined with the demands of the tournament, finally took their toll on me. In the 90th minute I went up for a head ball when our goalkeeper, Brianna Scurry, who was trying to clear the ball, punched me in the head. I went down in a heap but not necessarily because of the blow to my head. My body simply said, 'Okay, Mich, that is enough of that.' Although I tried to rally, my body was having nothing of it. The doctors took me into the training room to get treatment."

Akers has no recollection of the events that followed. Soccer's ultimate warrior doesn't remember being carried from the field or the ensuing penalty kicks that would determine the game's outcome. The medical staff began IVs on Michelle and administered oxygen while trying to determine whether or not they needed to send her to the emergency room. Watching the game's historic ending, Michelle was alert enough to see Brandi Chastain's Cup-winning goal.

"I slumped back with relief and joy that we had won and that, in my terms, my mission was accomplished," she recalls. "Immediately, I told the doctors to get the junk out of my arms so I could join my team to celebrate."

Akers wobbled out of the tunnel and made her way to

the medal podium to hug her teammates. She sat and rested while the others enjoyed a victory lap around the Rose Bowl. Soon she heard the cacophonous roar of thousands of fans chanting her name, "Akers! Akers! Akers!"

The moment moved her beyond words. She made her way to the middle of the field to respond to the throng with a wave, a smile, and a panoramic gaze at the unforgettable scene. She searched through the crowd, trying to spot her father. Her body was dead, but the rest of her had never felt more alive.

In the aftermath, the media hailed Michelle's performance as one of grit and guts. Coach DiCicco described Akers as having inspired the team and even him. President Clinton approached her in the locker room and told her, "From someone who knows how to take a hit, I admire you." And thousands of encouraging e-mails were sent to Akers' Web page.

The morning after the title game at the Rose Bowl, Akers woke up in her hotel room. She was still a mess, but she felt compelled to write something in her journal. She wrote, "I looked in the mirror last night and saw the weary face of a battle-worn soldier-warrior. But the eyes said it all. Exhausted, but fulfilled, satisfied. We did it."

Chicago's famous No. 50, Mike Singletary, 1989   Jonathan Daniel/Getty Images

MIKE SINGLETARY
ACING THE TEST

During a phenomenal 12-year career in the NFL, Mike Singletary became known in many circles as the greatest middle linebacker ever to play the game. When his career began, most experts thought he was too small and not physically gifted enough to make a difference in the league. Those experts were unable to measure Singletary's heart, however. The former Bears Hall of Famer built his career on intensity, preparation, and a strong belief he could accomplish anything if he worked at it hard enough.

The nine-time Pro Bowl selection and two-time NFL Defensive Player of the Year kept the same goal each year of his well-decorated career:

"I wanted to be the best player I could possibly be, so I could help my team be the best they could be."

Singletary was the best player on the best defense of his era—the 1985 Bears—who shut out two opponents in the playoffs and manhandled New England in Chicago's 46-10 victory in Super Bowl XX. This was Buddy Ryan's "46" defense, a complex, sophisticated scheme that depended greatly on the brain of Singletary, who was responsible for realigning his teammates in reaction to offensive changes.

"I looked at football and playing my position as a test," says Singletary. "Now, why wouldn't I get all the info I possibly could before I entered the game? By game time, I wanted to anticipate, remember, know everything I possibly could about the team—that would give me the edge."

To achieve this, Singletary became a student of the game. He devoted himself to never wasting a minute on the practice field. He threw himself into a strenuous conditioning

program in the off-season and continued to maintain that condition throughout the season. He spent hundreds of hours studying game film, to the point that once on the field he felt, in many situations, he knew what the opposing offense was about to do.

"Sometimes I felt Mike knew our plays better than some guys in my huddle," says former Detroit Lions quarterback Eric Hipple. "You could hear him calling out gaps that we were going to run through. I would audible, and he would counter. I believe he'd bait me, just to have me change the play so he could get me to run something he wanted."

"I looked at it as sort of a chess match," Singletary explains. "I'm out there, and I know when the quarterback comes to the line of scrimmage, there are things he's looking for and he's gonna audiblize and catch us at our weakest point. I'm going to counter that and call something that I feel puts our defense in our best position to attack the offense, and nine times out of ten, he's going to run out of time if he continues to audible. I'm always gonna have the defense in the best possible situation."

The '85 Bears were a team of characters epitomized by their music video "The Super Bowl Shuffle." Jim McMahon, Don Hampton, Otis Wilson, William (the Refrigerator) Perry, Steve McMichael, and others made for a colorful team. But Singletary was its heart and soul. It was his will to win, his sheer intensity that raised the Bears' level of quality to a nearly untouchable height. Even his wife, Kim, was stunned by the transformation that took place in this gentle man's persona once he took the field. She remembers being on the field before a game and walking by her husband.

"If it hadn't been for his number, I honestly would not have recognized him," she says.

"Middle linebacker, to me, is one of those things where you're involved physically, mentally, and spiritually as well," Singletary notes. "It takes everything you have to do it right. For me, the opportunity to go out there and let it go —when I left the field—I wanted everything to be left on the field. It was the greatest experience of my life."

All this from a guy who was told he would never make it in the NFL.

"The worst thing you can ever do is tell Mike he can't

do something," Kim says. "He has more self-confidence than anybody I've ever met. Sometimes too much."

Singletary once hired an agent only to discover he simply could walk into a corporate office himself, ask to see the president, and sell him on Mike Singletary. The approach worked so well that Singletary fired the agent and picked up more endorsements opportunities than he could possibly handle.

In 1984, when the Bears were on the verge of what had become, up to then, a typical collapse, Singletary took a stand. He gathered the team in the locker room and did his best to prepare them to give everything they had to make it to the playoffs.

"I refuse to go home early this year," he screamed. "I refuse. We are too good a team to go home early. I don't want to spend Christmas at home. I refuse to go home early." He preached for five minutes. Later, every time the team stumbled, the players would remember his tirade. They lost to San Francisco in the NFC Championship game that season but then went 15-1 in '85 and 14-2 in '86.

"That speech was the turning point of the Chicago

franchise," Ryan says.

"When I first played middle linebacker in the 7th grade," Singletary says, "my coach told me, 'You'll have to be the roughest guy on the field but still responsible for all the other guys on the field.' From then on, to me that was the role of middle linebacker—to assume leadership on the field."

Though he does not use it as an excuse, Mike grew up in a situation far different than the one he is making happen in his own family. He refers to it as the "Singletary Curse" because so many of his relatives have been affected by absentee fathers. His childhood was less than idyllic, and the memories drive him to provide a different atmosphere for his own family.

"But I never forget where I came from," he says. "I remember, after my parents were divorced, when it would rain and the water would pour into the sides of our house [in Houston] because the wood had rotted away and there was nothing there to keep it out except the blankets we'd put down. I wasn't much of an athlete. When they would choose sides on the playground, I'd be the last one taken.

That's why every time I have a chance now, I pick the left-out guy first. "Why did you take him?" people ask me, 'Because no one else will,' I tell them. I speak for those who can't speak, and I stand for those who can't stand for themselves."

Orel Hershiser against the Cubs, 1991   Jonathan Daniel /Allsport/Getty Images

OREL HERSHISER
REWRITING THE RECORD BOOK

In 1988, Orel Hershiser rewrote baseball's record books with all of the celebrity of a CPA. He looked like a choir boy but pitched with the heart of a lion. His amazing run thrust him into the national spotlight as one of the top pitchers in baseball as he led the Los Angeles Dodgers to an improbable World Championship in what remains one of the greatest single-season performances by a major league pitcher.

In his last 101 & 2/3 innings of that season, Hershiser was virtually unhittable, giving up a minuscule five earned runs, all of which came in 42 & 2/3 innings of postseason play—when he was starting on three days' rest. When

Sandy Koufax or Bob Gibson performed like men throwing to boys, they were considered demigods by their baffled opponents. But Hershiser's victims walked away shaking their heads, convinced they could hit him—if given just one more chance.

Maybe it's because he looked so unassuming. Maybe it's because he didn't stomp around the mound and glare at hitters, trying to intimidate them. Maybe it's because he never carried on a running dialogue with batters, challenging them to show who was more of a man. Maybe it's because he didn't posses a 95-mph fastball. Maybe it's because those pitches did look hittable until they sank, broke, sliced, or darted at the last moment. Maybe it's because after almost five years in the big leagues, Hershiser made a dramatic rise to elite status almost overnight.

Hershiser was Cy Young-like all of the '88 season, winning 23 games and losing 8, with a 2.26 ERA as the Dodgers won the National League West. He surpassed Hall of Famer Don Drysdale's mark by ending the regular season with a Major League record 59 consecutive scoreless innings. And he embodied the Dodgers' postseason Cinderella story, pitching and occasionally hitting L.A. to victory over the heavily favored New York Mets and

Oakland Athletics. More than that, he carried himself with remarkable grace and affability. While he was stunning on the mound, he also seemed a little stunned at what he was accomplishing. His humility touched a cord in many.

"One thing you have to remember about Orel," said former Dodgers' catcher Rick Dempsey, "is his determination. I've never seen anything like it. He wants to succeed so badly that he refuses to give in. He got into this groove, and he wasn't afraid to keep it going. Some guys will walk away from it because of the pressure, but he won't."

Hershiser never seemed to let the pressure rattle him. Through all the hoopla surrounding his achievements in '88, he always kept a sense of peace, which was visible to observers. In that year's World Series, in which the Dodgers upset the heavily favored A's, Oakland's young star Jose Canseco said that since he was only a third-year player, it was unfair to ask him to carry his team offensively. Hershiser knew his role, whether fair or not, and he embraced it and carried the Dodgers.

On the night of the Series-clinching game, he drove himself by "realizing that if I lost or didn't pitch well, people would say I cooled off just at the wrong time, when the team needed me the most, that I couldn't handle the pressure game. I didn't want that."

So through his tremendous discipline, Hershiser forced himself to focus only on the next pitch, the next batter, the next inning, and not what another superb performance could mean to him and his team.

That's how the famous hymns came about. Network television cameras caught Hershiser between innings, sitting on the bench, head back, eyes closed, seemingly meditating. But he wasn't meditating; he was singing. In between innings of the biggest game of his baseball life, Hershiser was singing some of his favorite hymns.

Said Hershiser, "I wanted to cleanse my mind of all the clutter in the world at that moment, to block out the pressure and concentrate on the game at hand."

His was the epitome of a Cinderella story, his triumph one for all who have been told they would never make it. Never could the Dodgers win the World Series. Never would Drysdale's record be broken. Never could this skinny kid become a Major League pitcher.

Hershiser's turnaround dates back to his freshman year at Bowling Green University. He had academic trouble and failed to make the baseball team's traveling squad. So he left campus for a few days and visited some old high school

Manager Tommy Lasorda congratulates Hershiser after a win over Oakland in the 1988 World Series. Focus on Sport/Getty Images

friends in his hometown of Cherry Hill, New Jersey, before hitchhiking back to school.

With new enthusiasm, Hershiser started hitting the books and made the dean's list. In his sophomore year, he grew three inches, added about five miles an hour to his fastball, and was finally good enough to crack the Falcons' traveling squad. Hershiser had disciplined himself to learn. And it set the tone for his professional future.

Upon his arrival in L.A. in 1994, Hershiser continued to learn. He would sit with manager Tommy Lasorda and pitching coach Ron Perranoski, soaking up everything they knew about pitching and the hitters in the National League. Much was made of Lasorda giving Hershiser the nickname "bulldog," but perhaps his real contribution to Hershiser's growth was the knowledge he imparted.

"Tommy taught me a lot about pitching," says Hershiser. "I didn't mind it if he second-guessed my pitch selection, because it was almost a Socratic method. 'Why did you throw that?' I would learn things like, 'don't throw off-speed to a left-hander with a man on first base, because he wants to hit the ball to the right side anyway.'"

The lessons took quickly. After a rookie season in which Hershiser was quickly moved from the bullpen to the

starting rotation, he soon became the Dodgers' ace. His commitment to learn and work was unparalleled. In his second season, he went 19-3 with a 2.03 ERA, setting the stage for his amazing run in '88.

Hershiser went on to pitch effectively through part of the 2000 season before he retired at the age of 41, having spent 18 years in the Major Leagues. He remains one of the most respected players ever to play the game, and his 1988 record has yet to be seriously challenged.

Tom Lehman   Jeff Gross/Getty Images

TOM LEHMAN

T om Lehman kept his perspective during a long journey from Minnesota and the mini-tours to the British Open and beyond. A late bloomer at each stage of his career—junior, college/amateur, and professional —Lehman was just learning to be a winner in one phase when it was time to move to the next. As a result, when he turned pro in 1982, he didn't have the confidence to make the normal progression that most tour stars do. It wasn't until 1992, after years of mini-tour play around the world, that he not only made it on the PGA Tour, but made it big.

In 1989, Lehman was practically broke. He had made no money to speak of as a golfer. He was down to his last $300, which he and his wife, Melissa, decided to spend on entering a tournament in South Africa, to give golf one last shot.

That last shot became a shot in the arm as Lehman won $30,000 at the tournament, setting off a new sense of confidence and a complete turnaround of his game. Among the upper echelon of players throughout the 1990s, Lehman was named player of the year in 1996 when he won over $1.7 million. His career earnings now exceed $7 million. So it seems that $300 was a good investment.

"I wouldn't trade those years for anything," says Lehman. "I look back and there's nothing but good memories. It was difficult. You really had to want to play golf and get good in order to go through it. You have got to do whatever it takes. So I look back at that and say, 'We did it.' Melissa and I together, we did whatever we had to do to get the job done. I just wanted to get as good as I could possibly get. I didn't care if I never got rich or famous. I wanted to play because I wanted to be good. And I always believed that I had the ability to be a really good player."

The lessons Lehman learned during the days he nearly quit have been put to good use now that he's established himself as a contender on the PGA tour.

Four times, Tom Lehman has played in the final group of the U.S. Open. Four times, he's watched someone else win.

For Lehman, the Open is more like open wounds. For four consecutive Junes—1995, 1996, 1997, and 1998—Lehman either held or shared the lead after three rounds. On each occasion, he ended up making a consolation speech to the media.

1996 provided the most interesting Open drama. For the final round, Lehman was paired with his friend and fellow Christian, Steve Jones. They were deadlocked after 71 holes, two pals on a stroll that would reward only one. Jones shot 69 and looked to the heavens. Lehman shot 71 and looked to next year—again.

But it is what happened en route to the final score that typifies Lehman's outlook on his 0-for-Opens. It was Lehman who kept Jones calm as he played in his first major championship since the 1991 British Open. He gave words of encouragement to Jones as they played together. He broke the ice as they walked down the first fairway.

"Twice during that final round, Tom quoted from the Book of Joshua to settle me down," Jones recalls. "He said, 'You know the Lord wants us to be courageous and strong, for that is the will of God.' I really got to thinking then. I said, 'Yeah, that is right.'

"If I saw Steve Jones just walking down the street at home, I would walk over, we'd talk, and I would say something nice to him," explains Lehman. "If I could encourage him in some way, I probably would. So if we are playing the last round of the U.S. Open, it shouldn't be any different. I should be able to walk up to Steve and say, 'Hey, Steve, I have got a [Bible] verse for you. I think it is pretty cool.' I would encourage him to be strong and courageous.

"He was nervous, I was nervous, but he hadn't been in that situation for a long time. He really needed to hear something to give him some peace. So I gave him that verse."

"Tom's day will come," says Jones.

"I've got a few years of good golf left in me, and if anything, all those close calls have reinforced my belief that I can win the Open. I haven't gotten to the point where I think it's not to be. It's the other way around, in fact. It's my kind of tournament. I really enjoy it. But the sooner, the better."

No one can question Lehman's tenacity, endurance, and determination. Says Jim Flick, his teacher since 1990: "There isn't anyone who learns from disappointments as much as Tom Lehman." To which Lehman replies, "I've had a lot more dealings with disappointment than the other extreme."

The disappointments include a heartbreaking loss at the 1994 Masters.

"That was always my greatest fear" Lehman notes. "To

die and have it written on my tombstone: Here Lies Tom Lehman, He Couldn't Win The Big One."

But a month after Jones' triumph in 1996—at Royal Lytham & St. Annes for the British Open—Jones willed all his birdies to Lehman. The prayers worked. Lehman led by six shots after 54 holes, and he finally won the major he least expected to win. Sometimes, even golf can be fair.

"Maybe when you deal with failure for so long, it tends to take a long time to overcome the idea you are a failure. The Hogan Tour [now Nike] was a huge step. Winning on the PGA Tour was another big step. Winning a major was the biggest step of all. So I see myself now as really being a champion. And yet, I know I am capable of being even better. I constantly have to work at giving myself enough credit for being a good player.

"A lot more people are going to go through the school of hard knocks than people who jump right in and are instant successes. Both ways are just fine. But I think more people can relate to going through some tough times before the good times."

"That is where you have to keep the balance in your life. You are a golfer, that's what you do. Obviously you want to be good, but there are things beyond golf that are far more important, and that is who you are on the inside."

John Elway drops back to pass during the 1987 AFC Championship Game against Cleveland. Bob Martin /Allsport/Getty Images

THE DRIVE

The Denver Broncos were on the 2-yard line—their own 2-yard line—with 5:32 left in the 1987 AFC Championship Game. The Cleveland Browns had just scored a go-ahead touchdown on their home field and held a 20-13 lead. They were just minutes away from their first trip to the Super Bowl. The "Dog Pound," Cleveland's Municipal Stadium, was rocking, with 79,915 fans celebrating so loudly that Broncos players could barely hear each other. With 98 yards to navigate, Denver's chances of a comeback looked slim.

Browns quarterback Bernie Kosar had just hit receiver Brian Brennan on a 48-yard touchdown pass. Then, on the ensuing kickoff, Denver's Ken Bell fumbled the ball and fell on it at the 2. The Browns had the momentum, and the Cleveland faithful let both teams know it.

Broncos players began to hang their heads after the botched kick return. Receiver Mark Jackson later admitted, "Everybody's emotions dropped when we realized we were at the 2, that we had 98 yards to go. You looked into your teammates' eyes, and you could see everyone thinking, 'Man, what else can go wrong?'"

But the Broncos still had hope, in a No. 7 jersey. Amidst the snow flurries on that frozen day, Denver quarterback John Elway, a master of the comeback, again trotted onto the field.

Elway smiled when he arrived in the huddle. Calmly and confidently, the four-year veteran looked downfield and then smiled again. "We've worked hard just to get to this point," he told his teammates. "We're 98 yards away. If we execute and work hard, just like we've done since August, good things will happen."

"He elevated all of us," receiver Steve Watson said later. "We were down after we fumbled the kickoff. We were tired. It was an ugly, cold day. But John made us believe. He made us believe that we could do it, that we had to do it.

Elway scans the Cleveland defense before the snap.   Bob Martin /Allsport/Getty Images

We hadn't moved the ball all day, and we were staring at a 98-yard drive. We were only in the game because the Browns committed some big turnovers. But all the doubts, all the questions disappeared when John got to the huddle."

On first down, Elway completed a five-yard pass to Sammy Winder. Winder then took a handoff and ran for three yards on second down. On third-and-2 from the 10, the crowd was so loud that Elway couldn't hear himself shout his own signals. He called timeout, but the crowd quieted only slightly. Elway conferred with coach Dan Reeves on the sideline. The two settled on a running play with Winder going over left guard. Winder picked up the first down, by inches, keeping the drive alive.

Elway huddled his team again near the 12-yard line. The fire in his eyes was unmistakable, yet his cool under pressure was evident to all his teammates. "I never saw him so calm," Broncos' receiver Vance Johnson would say later.

Elway was demonstrating the poise and form that would become his trademark—running, throwing darts from the pocket, or while scrambling—all under intense pressure.

On second and seven at the Denver 15, Elway was forced out of the pocket. Running on a bad ankle, he eluded tacklers and chugged for an 11-yard gain. Then, after getting sacked for an eight-yard loss, he was faced with a third-and-18 at the 18-yard line. Elway scrambled out of the pocket, scanned the field, and then hit Jackson for what was the crucial play of the drive—a 20-yard strike for a first down.

"I was going to take a shot downfield," Elway later said of the play, explaining that he knew Cleveland's safeties would be playing deep, enabling Jackson to find an open

seam. "It was just matter of me putting the ball there."

"Usually John gives that play a quick read, from the [deeper] route to the [shorter] route," Jackson added. "I was the guy who was 20 yards deep. If he wanted the first down, he'd be coming to me. I was bumped off the line. As I got to the top of the route, I broke and John had the ball right there. I didn't have too much time to think about it. John drilled me with the ball."

That play helped the Broncos regain some of the momentum. The crowd could feel things beginning to turn. Cleveland defensive players began to hang their heads. They did not know how to stop Elway. Reportedly, they looked at one another before each down and yelled, "Will someone stop him already?"

At the Cleveland 28, faced with a second-and-10, Elway hit Steve Sewell for 14 yards. The fans grew silent. In another second-and-10 situation at the Browns' 14, the quarterback scrambled for nine yards. As he slid hard over the sideline, Elway was hammered by a pair of Browns players, yet he jumped up and raced back to the huddle. The momentum was now all Denver's.

With a third-and-one at the 5-yard line, on the 15th play of the drive, Elway dropped back and threw a low rocket to Jackson running a slant pattern in the end zone. Jackson slid and caught the ball while on his knees, just across the goal line.

Elway had driven the Broncos 98 yards in just under five minutes to tie the game. He did it in a wind-chill temperature of 5 degrees and with a brutal wind blowing directly into his face. Thirty-seven seconds remained on the game clock. The stunned silence in the stadium could be sensed across Ohio.

Elway ran off the field knowing he had just engineered one of the greatest clutch drives in pro football history. It was a series of plays that became known simply as "The Drive."

The stats for The Drive: 78 yards passing, 20 yards rushing. Elway completed six of seven passes, with the one incompletion being a pass intentionally thrown out of bounds to stop the clock.

Elway completed the comeback in overtime by engineering another long drive, this one 60 yards, to set up kicker Rich Karlis for a short game-winning field goal. The Broncos won 23-20 and were headed to their first of what would be five Super Bowl appearances under Elway's leadership.

While the Broncos lost their first three Super Bowls,

Elway led them back to consecutive wins in 1998 and 1999, when they became only the sixth team ever to repeat as Super Bowl champions in consecutive years.

While Elway enjoyed many amazing performances during his Hall-of-Fame career, "The Drive" is the one achievement that defined him and set the stage for his future glory.

Mary Lou Retton at the Summer Olympics, Los Angeles, 1984   Steve Powell/Staff/Getty Images

AMAZING INDIVIDUAL PERFORMANCE

A PERFECT 10

The 1984 Summer Olympics in Los Angeles were a high point of athletic pride for the United States. Coming off a boycott of the 1980 Summer Games—a boycott that left the nation deflated, the USA dominated the '84 games, taking home a record 83 gold medals and 174 total medals.

No moment created more exhilaration for the USA than the performance of Mary Lou Retton in the women's gymnastics competition.

Retton was a commercial success in the making. She had a golden smile, a pixie haircut, and big, soft, brown eyes. Her youthful enthusiasm amidst a sea of near-robotic

Eastern Europeans captivated the world. The 16-year-old from Fairmont, West Virginia, stole America's heart. No American gymnast—male or female—had ever captured an Olympic gold medal in any portion of the competition. But Mary Lou was about to change that.

Early in the contest on the evening of August 3, 1984, Retton led all 36 other competitors in the all-around event. Romania's world champion Ecaterina Szabo trailed Retton by just 15 one-hundredths of a point. But Retton had two shaky landings during her balance beam routine, one on a forward flip and the other on a back walkover. She nailed her double somersaulting dismount, but her score was 9.80, and now she trailed Szabo by .15, with only the floor exercise and vault remaining.

Szabo, in the first spot throughout all four rotations, hit her first vault nearly perfectly, giving her a 9.90. Retton responded, turning in a flawless tumbling and dancing exhibition during her floor exercise. She scored a perfect 10, which narrowed Szabo's lead to .050 of a point—69.225 to 69.175.

Up first again on the uneven bars, Szabo was outstanding. But her score of 9.90 gave her a total of 79.125 points, which was not insurmountable. Retton knew she had a chance to win the gold. If she could stick either of her vaults and score another 10, she would win the gold by five hundredths of a point. She also knew that the slightest wobble would give her a 9.95, which would result in a tie for the gold. Anything less, and she would have to settle for silver. But for Retton, a 9.95 would not suffice. She was thinking only of the gold and had no intention of sharing it.

Retton reminded herself that she always vaulted best under pressure. The scrappy teenager set her mind and heart on nothing short of the perfect vault. "I kept thinking stick, stick, stick," she would say later. "I knew I had to get a 10."

From the side of the platform, Retton's coach, Bela Karolyi, encouraged her. Before he could give her any advice, Retton looked at him and said, "I'm going to stick it." Karolyi flashed a big grin. "Stick it" in gymnastics means landing so firmly and solidly that a gymnast "sticks" to the mat without even as much as a wobble.

As she walked to her place at the end of the approach, Retton was not thinking about her right knee, which had required arthroscopic surgery for the removal of torn cartilage just two months before the games began. Instead, she was remembering the day she had stretched out on the floor of her family room eight years earlier and watched Romania's Nadia Comaneci win the all-around gold medal at the 1976 Games in Montreal. Retton was captivated by that moment. She remembered thinking, *I want that to be me.* Now it was time to fulfill that dream.

The 9,023 fans that packed UCLA's Pauley Pavilion were completely silent as Retton prepared to make her run at the gold. She sprinted the 73-1/2 feet to the board and launched herself high into the air. She twisted her body, then hit the vault horse and pushed off, thrusting herself into a perfect backward somersault in a laid-out position with a full twist, 360 degrees, and then stuck the landing, coming to a stop in the center of the mat, upright and still. Not one wobble. It was an amazing effort, a 10.

As they waited to see Retton's score posted, the sellout crowd began to chant, "TEN ... TEN ... TEN." Within seconds, the bright, bold "10" flashed on the small electronic scoreboard near the vault area. The crowd went wild, knowing they had witnessed the first American to ever win a gold medal in an Olympic gymnastics competition.

As the score was posted, Retton leaped into the air, held her arms up to heaven, smiled, waved, and blew kisses to the crowd. She had captured the gold. But she had to

briefly interrupt her celebration to comply with the rule that a gymnast must do two vaults, with the higher score prevailing. So, back to the approach she went. She sprinted to the board and vaulted. Once again, Retton delivered a flawless maneuver, and once again, she stuck the landing. The scoreboard flashed another 10. The crowd again went wild, this time outdoing their earlier effort, chanting "USA! USA! USA!" and "Mary Lou! Mary Lou! Mary Lou!"

Retton won the gold and the hearts of the American people. She became the heroine of the 1984 Summer Games. She also became the darling of American gymnastics, the standard by which all gymnasts would forever be measured, all on the strength of one electrifying night in L.A. in 1984.

Dan Jansen, victorious in the 1000 meters, Lillehammer, 1994
Chris Cole/ALLSPORT/Getty Images

A CHAMPION GETS UP

The years of heartbreak and misery had stayed with Dan Jansen. It was difficult for him not to feel like a failure.

But on a special night in Lillehammer, Norway, at the 1994 Winter Olympics, what seemed like a lifetime of disappointment and sorrow all drifted away in a span of one minute, 12 seconds, and 43 hundredths of a second. In the end, the agony of the previous ten years seemed worth it for Jansen. Suddenly it all had purpose and meaning.

During the 1980s and '90s, Jansen was considered the best speed skater in the world. He had established several world records while winning world championships and World Cup competitions. The only major title he had not captured was a medal in the Olympics, his sport's highest honor. In Sarajevo in 1984, Calgary in 1988, and Albertville in 1992, he was zero for six in both the 500 and 1,000-meter races. He was a man without a medal. On each occasion, disaster hit in the form of one mishap or another.

Calgary was the most difficult for Jansen. On the day of the 500-meter race, he received word that his older sister, Jane, had died of leukemia. With the world rooting for him, a grief-stricken Jansen, the gold-medal favorite, fell and did not finish. That evening in the 1,000 meters, once again with the world cheering him on, he also fell.

Four years later, in the Albertville Games, redemption did not come as everyone expected. Jansen lost his balance in a turn in the 500 and finished fourth. Fans began to wonder if Jansen was cursed. Later that day, he staggered across the finish line of the 1,000—in 26th place, and the world was heartbroken again with him.

He had one last chance at the '94 Olympics in Lillehammer. He was 28, somewhat old for his sport. Younger legs had steadily gained on him. This would be his

last shot at a medal. He was the favorite to win the 500, which had always been his best event. Yet, Jansen amazingly and agonizingly slipped again and finished eighth.

He went into the 1,000 meters, the final Olympic race of his career, with low expectations. By then he was almost afraid to hope, thinking he would only be setting himself up for more disappointment.

When he took the ice at Hamar's Vikingskipet Skating Hall before a capacity crowd, he lined up against seven competitors—all of whom had better times than his career best in the event. To make matters worse, his timing had been off during warm-ups as he struggled to gain traction on the ice.

As he prepared to set off on his final chance for a medal, Jansen knew he had to skate at least three-tenths of a second faster than he had ever before—just to match his competition. In the back of the minds of all viewers were the lingering questions: When will disaster strike this time? How will it happen? Where will he slip and fall? It was as if this had become the expectation for all observers. Perhaps even for Jansen.

With one hand behind his back, the other swinging at

his side, Jansen made it to the next-to-last turn without a problem. He was skating in the inner lane, where the turn is tighter and the chance of a fall greater. And he was fatigued. Suddenly, he slipped ever so slightly. His left hand grazed the ice, just barely. But just when the watching world was prepared to see him hit the ice, this time, somehow, Jansen stayed on his feet. He lost two or three hundredths of a second, but still kept his rhythm and balance. "For some reason I was calm when I slipped," he said later. "There was no panic."

As Jansen hit the straightaway, the fans rose to their feet, frenzied as they watched him fly down the stretch and cross the finish line. The clocks read 1:12.43—a new world record.

Jansen raised his arms to the heavens, pulled his head back as if to look up to the sky, shut his eyes, and then dropped his hands on his head in disbelief. As applause erupted all around him, Jansen said to himself, "Finally! Finally!"

When his time flashed on the scoreboard, showing his first-place finish, his wife and mother screamed and hugged. Jansen's wife was so overcome with emotion that

she hyperventilated and had to be rushed to an emergency medical station for treatment.

"I feel I've made other people happy instead of having them feel sorry for me," Jansen said later. "I was

Dan Jansen after his fall in the 1000-meter race in Calgary, 1988 Toshio Sakai/AFP/Getty Images

thinking, just skate. I figured this was going to be my last Olympic race ever, no matter what happened. Winning here was the only thing left for me to do. It seems like I had to quit caring too much to skate my best."

As Jansen stood atop the center podium, had the gold medal placed around his neck, and listened to the national anthem, tears rolled from his eyes. "I was shaking," Jansen admitted. "I kept saying, 'I can't believe this.'" When the anthem ended, he looked upward and extended a personal salute to his sister Jane.

After leaving the podium, Jansen skated the Lap of Honor, as is customary in Europe. The arena lights were dimmed and a spotlight framed him while the crowd sang along to Strauss's "Viennese Waltz." Someone threw Jansen a Dutch flag. Then an American flag. Then a bouquet of flowers. Then a large Styrofoam wedge of Swiss cheese that sports fans in Jansen's home state of Wisconsin wear on their heads at athletic events.

While Jansen basked in the affection of the skating community, a security guard passed Jansen's daughter Jane —named after his late sister—over the heads of photographers and into Jansen's arms. With the spotlight shining on

him, Jansen held his daughter and carried her around the rink in a celebration that seemed to wipe away the past. It was a moment in which people from around the world were brought together for a special outpouring of emotion fit for a true champion.

An exhausted Kellen Winslow is helped from the field.

THE GAME NO
ONE SHOULD LOSE

The 1982 American Football Conference division playoff battle that pitted the San Diego Chargers against the Miami Dolphins was a game that neither team should have lost. It was played at Miami's Orange Bowl on January 2 to determine who would advance to the AFC Championship. But more than providing a winner, it was a platform for heroic effort. The epic battle is considered one of the greatest games in league history. It lasted 4 hours and 45 minutes and left 90 players dragging their bodies off the field when it ended.

The game began as a rout. San Diego quickly jumped to a 24-0 lead, but the Dolphins rallied to tie the game by halftime. The Chargers regained the lead in the third quarter, 31-24, on a touchdown pass from quarterback Dan Fouts to tight end Kellen Winslow. The Dolphins came right back when backup quarterback Don Strock, playing for injured starter David Woodley, hit tight end Bruce Hardy for a 50-yard TD pass. The game was again tied, 31-31.

By this time, the Miami heat and humidity made the Orange Bowl feel like a sauna. Players from both teams began to wilt. The game turned into a war of attrition.

In the fourth quarter, Dolphins' safety Lyle Blackwood intercepted Fouts to set up a short touchdown by running back Tony Nathan, giving Miami a 38-31 lead.

By the time Miami forced the Chargers to punt on their next possession, many players were gasping for air and water. Chargers All-Pro tight end Winslow was barely able to walk to the sideline. He had cramps in his thigh, both calves, and his lower back, making it difficult for him to stand. "I felt paralyzed," he said later. The Chargers star had entered the game with a bruised left shoulder, a strained right rotator cuff, and a sore neck. Because of these injuries, he had needed help from teammates just to put on his

shoulder pads before the game.

Now, with the game deep into the fourth quarter, Winslow looked spent. He had to be helped to the bench by teammates. Trainers surrounded him, massaging his calves and back and pouring fluids into his mouth. Still, in a show of courage that sets the great athletes apart from the rest, Winslow summoned the will to keep playing.

With five minutes to play and Miami leading 38-31, Strock led a long drive down the field that ate up the clock and moved the Dolphins to the San Diego 21-yard line. Trying to set up a game-winning field goal, Strock handed the ball to fullback Andra Franklin who plunged up the middle into a wall of Chargers. As Franklin fell to the ground, the ball was stripped from him by San Diego nose tackle Louie Kelcher. San Diego had the ball and one last chance.

The Miami defense took the field with little energy left to chase the explosive Chargers' offense. Fouts was given plenty of time to throw and put together a great drive — connecting with Charlie Joiner for 14 yards, Wes Chandler for six, Joiner for five, and then Joiner again for 15 more. He then hit Winslow for seven and Chandler for 19, which brought the ball to the Miami 9-yard line.

On first-and-goal, Fouts dropped back, scrambled,

and lobbed the ball toward the back corner of the end zone to Winslow. The fatigued tight end jumped but couldn't get a hand on the ball. After it sailed over Winslow, the ball dropped into the waiting hands of Chargers' rookie running back James Brooks, who had run to the back line of the end zone behind Winslow—just in case. Brooks grabbed the ball for the tying touchdown with 55 seconds left. "One of the all-time brilliant heads-up plays," Fouts told the media after the game. "In the hundreds of times we'd run that play, I'd never thrown to anybody back there."

On the ensuing kickoff, Chargers coach Don Coryell called for a squib kick, hoping the Dolphins would fumble. Fouts tried to talk his coach out of it, wanting to bury the Dolphins deep in their own territory. Coryell went with the squib kick. The Dolphins handled the kick and started at their own 40, with 52 seconds left.

Strock's first-down pass was nearly picked off. His second pass was intercepted by cornerback Willie Buchanon, who promptly fumbled the ball right back to Miami. The Dolphins drove into field-goal range with four seconds left and called timeout. Kicker Uwe von Schamann, the AFC's most accurate field goal kicker during the regular season, came on to attempt a 43-yard field goal.

Winslow, who had almost passed out on the bench merely trying to hold down liquids, rose and slowly walked back onto the field to try to block the kick. He had never blocked a field goal in his career. Hardly able to stand, he was just hoping he could somehow get his 6-6 frame in the way of the kick and deflect it. His teammates tried to prevent him from going on the field, but Winslow pushed them aside and marched on.

"Get me some penetration," Winslow yelled to his teammates. As the ball was kicked, Winslow gathered enough strength to leap in the air and tip it with the pinkie finger on his right hand. The field goal attempt, deflected, was no good. The game went into overtime.

After blocking the field goal, Winslow stretched out on the ground, unable to move. He was carried off the field in agony. Coryell went into overtime thinking that Winslow was unavailable. Amazingly, however, the Chargers' tight end made his way back onto the field after San Diego won the coin toss and received the kickoff.

The Chargers moved downfield quickly, the tired Dolphins defense unable to do much of anything to stop them. Coryell called on Rolf Benirschke to kick a 27-yard field goal. Benirschke hadn't missed from inside 30 yards all year. But a tired Charger field goal unit was late getting onto the field, forcing a quick snap. With his rhythm off, Benirschke hooked his kick left. The game went on, deep into the night.

With the score tied at 38-38 and nine minutes expired in overtime, Strock moved Miami downfield to set up another von Schamann field goal attempt, this time a 34-yarder. Across the field, Benirschke kneeled on the sideline. "It was like watching your own execution," he said later. Incredibly, von Schamann missed again.

Fouts drove San Diego downfield, hitting Brooks and Chandler each twice in a row, then connecting with Joiner for 39 yards. The Chargers were poised to score at the Miami 10. Benirschke was presented with another chance. The kick was perfect, ending the epic battle.

As the scoreboard flashed the final, San Diego 41, Miami 38, players from both teams lay exhausted on the field. As they all struggled to their feet, the valiant Winslow, who caught 16 passes for 166 yards, took three steps and fell flat on the ground. His body temperature had risen to 105 degrees. He had to be helped to the locker room by two teammates who practically carried him off the field. It was later revealed that Winslow lost 13 pounds during the game.

Like a heavyweight title fight between two great champs, this game was a matter of the winner being the last one standing. An amazing effort by Winslow represented the heart of the players who made this a game considered by many to be the greatest in NFL history.

Doug Flutie celebrates the win over the Hurricanes.   The Miami Herald/Joe Rimkus, Jr.

THE HAIL MARY

One of the most memorable moments in college football would never have happened if not for the work of some creative television executives.

It was a classic David and Goliath matchup. Goliath was 6' 5" Heisman Trophy candidate quarterback Bernie Kosar and his defending NCAA champion Miami Hurricanes. David was underdog Boston College's 5' 10" Heisman hopeful quarterback, Doug Flutie. The 1984 showdown had major implications not only for the Heisman, but also for that year's bowl games. It was a matchup that had television executives drooling. The game had originally been scheduled for September 29, but to optimize its TV ratings, the execs wanted to move it closer to the end of the season. They decided on the evening of Friday, November 23, the day after Thanksgiving. But some serious convincing was required in order to move the game. Miami had been scheduled to play Rutgers on that date, so the network went to work and convinced the schools to rearrange the schedule. Rutgers, for a fee of $80,000, canceled its game with Miami. The Miami versus BC game was on.

By late season, Flutie had become a media darling. The undersized player showed a huge heart, leading Boston College to national prominence and setting himself up to become college football's first 10,000-yard career passer. "Flutie magic" had been at work all year, and thousands of fans wondered if he could pull off an upset of Kosar's champs. The game was everything fans expected. The sold-out crowd at Miami's Orange Bowl witnessed an electrifying offensive shootout. For nearly four hours, the two teams went back and forth down the field. There were 15 scoring drives, none of less than 55 yards—with five of them covering 80 yards or more. The teams combined for 1,273 yards in total offense.

At halftime, Boston College led 28-21. Then, as in a scene from a movie, a heavy tropical rainstorm hit the area and began pelting the stadium while the teams were off the field. Enduring the rain, Miami opened the second half with a 96-yard drive to tie the game at 28. The teams then exchanged field goals, and the game remained tied at 31-31 as the fourth quarter began. A Boston College field goal broke the tie, but Miami took the lead with a Melvin Bratton 52-yard touchdown run. With 3:50 remaining in the game, BC again drove down the field, 82 yards, to take a 41-38 lead.

With 2:30 left to play, Miami began a drive of its own and scored on another Bratton run, putting the Hurricanes on top 45-41 with 28 seconds left on the clock. As Bratton crossed the goal line, Miami's players went wild, thinking they had finally put BC away. "I thought we had it won," Miami center Ian Sinclair later told the media. "We all did."

"I assumed we had lost," Boston College coach Jack Bicknell admitted afterward. "I'm thinking, 'What am I going to tell these guys in the locker room? They just played a great game.'"

Flutie may have been the only one in the stadium who wasn't thinking the game was over. As he watched the Miami sideline celebration, he began to think through what plays he would run once his team got the ball back. Flutie calculated in his head that his Golden Eagles could run four plays if they managed the remaining 28 seconds well. He envisioned getting the ball to midfield in two plays and then taking a shot at the end zone. As he entered the huddle for the first play following the kickoff, Flutie yelled to his teammates over the din of the crowd, "OK, let's get near midfield. If we can get it there, we have a 50-50 chance of scoring."

Starting at his own 20 yard line, Flutie picked up 19 yards on a pass to Troy Stradford. On the next play, he completed a pass to Scott Gieselman for 13 more yards to get into Miami territory. The ball rested on the Hurricanes' 48 yard line with 10 seconds left on the clock. Flutie's next pass fell incomplete. With six seconds remaining, Boston had 48 yards to cover and just one play to make it happen. In the huddle, Flutie looked into the eyes of his teammates and called "Flood Tip," a play in which three receivers run downfield, congregate in (or "flood") one area at the end zone, and try to catch Flutie's pass. The play was designed for Flutie's main receiver, Gerard Phelan. If Phelan was unable to catch the ball, he was supposed to tip it to one of the other two receivers. The team had practiced the play especially for situations like this. They had also run it three times in games. It worked once, earlier in the 1984 season, with Phelan catching a touchdown pass at the end of the

first half against Temple. Flutie and Phelan relived that play in their minds as the Eagles broke the huddle.

Flutie took the snap and dropped back to pass. Miami All-American defensive lineman Jerome Brown broke through the pass protection and chased Flutie out of the pocket. As Flutie stepped forward to throw, he saw Hurricane defensive end Willie Broughton heading straight at him. Now back at his own 37 yard line, Flutie reared back and heaved the ball toward the end zone. The ball cut straight into a 30-mile-per-hour wind and sailed some 60 yards downfield.

Miami's defensive coaches had called a deep prevent defense in which three defensive backs were assigned to protect the end zone. Apparently unaware of Flutie's arm strength, the three Hurricanes positioned themselves near the 10-yard line, ready to make a play. But Phelan was able to slip behind them and get to the goal line. "I didn't know Phelan was behind us," Darrell Fullington later told the media. "I took my eye away from him for just one second to see where Flutie was, and it was too late. I looked back, and the ball was in the air and Phelan was past me. I jumped as hard as I could, but...."

Flutie's pass sailed through the wet evening air just

beyond the reach of the Miami defenders. As Fullington tried to recover and quickly get back toward the end zone, he ran into teammate Reggie Sutton. While Fullington and Sutton teetered off-balance at the 3-yard line, the ball dropped just over their outstretched arms and right into Phelan's hands.

Sixty yards away, Flutie was stretched out on the ground, staring up at the sky, courtesy of Broughton, with no idea how the play finished. When he picked himself off the turf and realized what had happened, he ran toward the end zone, waving his arms wildly, ecstatically jumping and turning in circles all the way. "I thought the pass fell incomplete," he said later. "When I saw the referee's arms go up in the air for a touchdown, I could not believe it."

What Flutie had seen as he began his jaunt toward his celebrating teammates was Phelan—at the bottom of a pile of Boston College players—still holding on to his 11th catch of the game, cradling it as he would later say, "as if it were my first-born." On the sidelines, on the field, and in the stands, BC players and fans went crazy over the play that would become known as the "Miracle in Miami." It was replayed over and over on highlight shows across America for the next week and became one of the most

memorable plays in college football history. It locked up the Heisman Trophy for Flutie and established the diminutive quarterback's place among the great college quarterbacks of all time.

Dwight Clark's fingertip catch tied the 1981 NFC Championship Game with 51 seconds left on the clock. Bruce Bennett Studios/Getty Images

AMAZING HEROICS

THE CATCH

"The Catch" has become known as one of the greatest plays in NFL history. It was so crucial that few remember that it came not in a Super Bowl, but in an NFC Championship Game. Still, the importance of the moment and the improbability of the play make "The Catch" one of the most memorable moments ever.

It was a play the San Francisco 49ers had practiced every day, from the first day of training camp through the end of the regular season. However, as they continued to practice it in preparation for their playoff tilt against the Dallas Cowboys, the players wondered why the coaching staff insisted they work on the play. Most 'Niners players, including Joe Montana, wished the "Sprint Right Option" could be deleted from the playbook. "We hated it," Montana said.

The play forced Montana to roll out, then leap into the air and throw the ball. It seemed each time Montana attempted the throw in practice, San Francisco coach Bill Walsh would tell him to throw the ball harder and higher. Disgustedly, Montana would shake his head and wonder why he was spending so much time on a play that seemingly would never be used in a game.

But in the waning moments of the 1982 NFC Championship Game on January 10, Montana and his 49ers teammates would all be thankful Walsh had paid so much attention to that one play.

The Dallas Cowboys had come to San Francisco's Candlestick Park for what would become an epic showdown between two of football's powerhouse teams. Only one would earn the right to call itself NFC Champion and have a chance for Super Bowl rings. Rain earlier in the week had left the playing surface at Candlestick muddy and turned the game into a match of power and leverage. The lead changed hands six times throughout the contest. With just 4:54 left on the clock, the Cowboys clung to a 27-21

lead as the 49ers took possession of the ball on their own 11 yard line.

As the 49ers began to move the ball at the start of the drive, a proverbial chess match between coaching geniuses began on the sidelines. Dallas coach Tom Landry, convinced Montana would throw on nearly every down, abandoned his famed "flex" defense in favor of nickel coverage—which positioned six defensive backs and one linebacker in pass coverage. Across the field, Walsh decided to counter by changing his game plan, eschewing his two-minute-offense passing game and keeping the ball on the ground. The 49ers began to grind out small chunks of yardage with a series of runs.

Then, just prior to the two-minute warning, Walsh again changed his scheme. Montana went to the air and hit fullback Earl Cooper with a short pass. The 49ers crossed midfield and, in the process, confused the Cowboys' defense. Walsh added to the confusion after the two-minute warning by calling a double-reverse with the ball going to wide receiver Freddie Solomon, who picked up 14 yards to the Dallas 35. Next, Montana hit Dwight Clark with a 10-yard pass and then Solomon for 12 yards. San Francisco reached the Dallas 13 with just over a minute remaining.

The hometown fans were nearly delirious as they realized all that stood between their beloved 49ers and their first Super Bowl appearance was a mere 13 yards.

Montana tried to hit Solomon in the end zone, but the pass was long. Then the 'Niners again surprised the Cowboys with a running play. Halfback Lenvil Elliott went over left tackle, slicing his way to the Dallas six. Facing third down and three yards to go with 58 seconds left, Walsh called a timeout. At the sideline, Walsh calmly told his quarterback to run "Sprint Right Option," the play Montana hated. There was no debate. Montana trotted back to the huddle and called the play. At the line of scrimmage, Montana had both receivers, Solomon and Dwight Clark, wide to the right. Solomon's job was to screen Dallas cornerback Emerson Walls, who was playing man-to-man on Clark. The design of the play was to free Clark to get open on the other side of the field. As Montana took the snap and dropped back to pass, Solomon slipped and could not get away from Dallas safety Dennis Thurman. However, Solomon recovered quickly and was eventually able to occupy Walls' attention for a split second—just long enough to give Clark some room to get free.

Montana rolled to his right, scanning the field, first

Montana celebrates as the 'Niners defeat the Cowboys for the NFC Championship.
Bruce Bennett Studios/Getty Images

looking over the middle and then focusing on the right side at the back of the end zone. Montana, forced toward the right sideline by heavy pressure from Dallas defensive tackle Ed "Too Tall" Jones and linebacker D.D. Lewis, was running out of room.

Clark, seeing his quarterback's situation, turned from his pattern and ran toward the back corner of the end zone. With just a step left before he was run out of bounds, Montana spotted Clark and jumped and lofted the ball—hard and high—toward his receiver.

Walls, who had already intercepted Montana twice in the game, trailed Clark but seemed convinced that the ball would sail over Clark's head and through the end zone. In fact, many who witnessed the scene were certain Montana, about to be forced out of bounds for a loss, was simply trying to throw the ball away. But the 6' 4" Clark leaped into the air, stretching out to perform a seemingly impossible feat. Reaching high over Walls, Clark grasped the ball with his fingertips before cradling it in his hands and landing on his feet in the corner of the end zone. As Clark slammed the ball into the turf in celebration, amazed fans sorted out what they had just seen. Seconds later, Ray Wersching's point-after-touchdown split the uprights and the score read

San Francisco 28, Dallas 27, with just 51 seconds to play.

A stunned Cowboys team made a futile, last-gasp attempt to move the ball, but the Niners held on to win. As the gun sounded, signifying the game's end, fans poured onto the field and mobbed Clark and Montana. They had witnessed "The Catch," the amazing play that sent the 49ers to their first Super Bowl.

Cal's Kevin Moen collides with the Stanford band and wins the game.
© 1982 Robert Stinnet

THE TROMBONE
DEFENSE

For a century, the Stanford-California rivalry has been one of the more spirited in all of college football. Each year, passionate San Francisco Bay Area fans argue over who will win The Big Game. There is, however, no argument over which Stanford-Cal contest is the Biggest of All of the "Big" Games. It occurred on November 20, 1982, at Memorial Stadium on the University of California-Berkeley campus.

Four seconds showed on the clock after Stanford place-kicker Mark Harmon booted a field goal to put

Stanford in the lead, 20-19. All-American quarterback John Elway had led the Cardinal downfield in the game's waning moments on a drive that ended in Harmon's kick, apparently snatching a victory away from the Bears. A crowd of 80,000 had been treated to a great football game. Many fans began to leave the stadium, unaware that they were about to be treated to the most famous (or, perhaps, infamous) play in college football history. While the teams prepared for what appeared to be a meaningless kickoff, Cal senior Kevin Moen was so upset over Harmon's apparent game-winning field goal that he refused to join the Cal return team's huddle prior to the kick. He missed teammate Richard Rodgers' plea to his teammates to "pitch the ball back and forth, to keep the play alive, no matter what."

Moen rushed onto the field just in time to get in position for Harmon's kickoff. Rodgers yelled to him, "Keep the play alive!" Harmon, under the instruction of Stanford coach Paul Wiggin, was to execute a squib kick, keeping the ball bouncing on the ground and making it difficult for Cal players to pick it up.

Harmon's kick bounced and rolled to Moen, who fielded it at the Cal 43-yard line. He immediately looked toward Rodgers, who was near the sideline, and then threw an overhand pass to him. Rodgers grabbed the toss and began to weave his way through members of the Stanford kickoff team, heading upfield. When he was surrounded by Cardinal players, Rodgers stopped and pitched the ball to freshman running back Dwight Garner. Garner quickly cut to his left toward the Cal sideline. As he neared midfield, four Stanford players came at him from both sides. Just as Garner was about to be hit, he turned his body away from the defenders and away from the closest referee.

Tacklers began to corral him, and as Garner started to fall toward the turf, his knee appeared to touch the field, which would have ended the play. While replays following the game seemed to confirm Garner's knee did hit the ground, no official blew a whistle. The officials closest to the play had their view obscured by Stanford players.

Then, the ball suddenly came flying out from the scrum. Garner had somehow twisted backward to get rid of the ball at the last possible moment, tossing it back to Rodgers. Official Jack Langley said after the game that he was ready to blow the play dead when he saw the ball come out. "I didn't see Garner get tackled, and I didn't see his knee hit the ground," he explained. "All I saw was the ball come flying out."

Three laterals had been successful and, incredibly, the play was still alive. Rodgers circled back toward the middle of the field, eluding several Stanford players. He crossed midfield and headed toward an opening on the right side. Cal receiver Mariet Ford shadowed Rodgers, just a few yards off of his outside shoulder. Rodgers tossed the ball to Ford at the Stanford 45-yard line. The speedy receiver then broke into the open field and headed toward the end zone. The crowd began to stir, recognizing that something amazing might be unfolding before them. Ford raced past Stanford players all the way to the 28. Trailing behind him was Moen, the man who had started the play with the first lateral. As a pair of Stanford players converged on Ford, he jumped into the air and, as he slammed into them, blindly flipped the ball over his shoulder into the waiting hands of Moen at the 27 yard line—for successful lateral number five. "I don't know how I knew Kevin was there; I just knew he was there," Ford said of the toss. "My goal was to take out the Stanford guys in front of me and hope my pitch stayed in the air long enough for Kevin."

Meanwhile, as the crazy series of laterals unfolded, the Stanford band, thinking the game was over, had begun to step onto the field through the Cal end zone. As Moen grabbed the ball, he saw a sea of trumpets, drums, and cymbals in front of him. Making it into the end zone meant he would not only have to outmaneuver the Stanford football team, but also get past the school's band. Moen, who had never scored a touchdown in his four years as a Bear, told himself, "Just put your head down and go to the end zone."

He dodged several band members at the five yard line, then crossed the goal line, where he leaped into the air and crashed into unsuspecting trombone player Gary Tyrrell, knocking him to the ground.

Pandemonium ensued as both teams attempted to sort out what they had just experienced. No one in the stadium knew if Stanford had won the game 20-19, or if Cal had taken it by a score of 25-20. As the crowd quieted, the officials huddled to confer about the play. After a few moments, the referee raised his arms, indicating a Cal touchdown and a 25-20 Bears victory. Those tuned in on radio heard Cal announcer Joe Starkey sum it up well: "The Bears have won! Oh my God! The most amazing, sensational, dramatic, heart-rending, exciting, thrilling finish in the history of college football!"

Ken Griffey Jr. at bat, 2004   John Grieshop/MLB Photos/Getty Images

AMAZING HEROICS

THE CALLED SHOT

Professional athletes are often portrayed as greedy individuals who care for little more than paychecks and endorsements. But in 2004, one of baseball's biggest stars showed his heart in a moment that touched the life of a very special family.

Kenny Marino was a New York City firefighter who died in the September 11 terrorist attack on the World Trade Center. He was also a big baseball fan and, in particular, a fan of Cincinnati Reds' outfielder Ken Griffey Jr. When Griffey learned about Marino, he was determined to do something to reach out to the deceased fireman's family.

Before one of the Reds' first games following the 9-11 tragedy, Marino's widow, Katrina, e-mailed Reds' public relations director, Rob Butcher, with the following message:

"My husband, Kenny Marino, a Rescue 1 firefighter, is missing. Ken Griffey Jr. was his favorite player. . . . If Ken Griffey Jr. could hit an extra home run for Kenny, I know he will be looking down with a big smile."

Griffey was moved—and he delivered—belting a home run in the Reds' 8-1 victory over the Philadelphia Phillies that night.

Griffey had briefly met Kenny Marino while still playing for the Seattle Mariners. Marino attended a Mariners-Yankees game in New York and got close enough to the field to give Griffey an NYFD (New York Fire Department) T-shirt for Griffey's son, Trey. "We still have the shirt," Griffey said.

After his gift home run in response to Katrina's first e-mail, Griffey began communicating regularly with the Marino family. He continued to bless the Marino children with notes and gifts. In 2004, he made the Marinos his special guests for a Reds game against the New York Mets at Shea Stadium. Katrina and her two children, Kristen and Tyler, visited with Griffey in the Reds' dugout. Kristin was on his

shoulders. Tyler was crawling on his lap. Kristin took off Griffey's hat and tried it on. "He's been so nice," Katrina said of Griffey. "The kids have really taken to him, and he's taken to them as well. You can tell he's a family person."

Unlike Babe Ruth's supposed "Called Shot" some 75 years earlier, Griffey's homer was unquestionably in response to a hopeful request. And Griffey went beyond the homer to reach out to a family who had lost so much. Through Griffey's kindness, the family gained a new friend. For Katrina Marino, being able to visit with Griffey at Shea created a bright, happy, memorable day following too many bad ones. "I didn't know it would affect me so much," she said, fighting back tears. "This would have meant so much to Kenny."

Pete Maravich   Nancy Hogue/NBAE/Getty Images

AMAZING RECORD BREAKERS

THE PISTOL

Pete Maravich was a skinny kid with shaggy hair and floppy socks who single-handedly revolutionized the game of basketball.

As a shooter, his range was unlimited—anywhere from inside the gym seemed possible.

As a passer, he had no equal. Pistol Pete's passes were never ordinary. Behind the back, through the legs, off the elbow, around the head . . . over the river and through the woods to basketball iconism he went.

Simply put, Maravich did things no one had ever seen before. Circus shots, slick moves, and passes the likes of which hadn't even been dreamed of before. When he played, it was the pure showtime—the joy of improvising in a game of formality that showcased his talent and considerable nerve. Make a mistake and he'd look like a fool. But Pete didn't care. When he was on the court, the night was his. He came to play and played to please.

On the night of January 31, 1970, Maravich pleased everyone in attendance when he broke the most storied record in college basketball and became the game's all-time leading scorer.

Maravich had averaged an amazing 43.8 points per game as a sophomore and 44.2 per game as a junior. With 14 games left in his senior season at Louisiana State University, he needed just 40 points to break Oscar Robertson's NCAA career scoring record of 2,973 points. During that January home game in Baton Rouge, Louisiana, against Mississippi, the Pistol took aim at the mark.

The slender 6' 5" guard scored 25 points . . . in the first half. And when he hit a 23-foot jump shot from the corner with 4:42 left in the game, he had the record. The overflow crowd of more than 11,000 in the LSU Coliseum went wild. The game

was stopped, and the game ball was given to Maravich.

Pistol Pete went on to score 12 more points in the final minutes of LSU's 109-86 victory. He finished the game with 53 points, giving him 2,987 over the course of two seasons.

In the week following the milestone against Mississippi, Maravich set two more marks. On February 2, he surpassed the 3,000-point mark, and on February 7 he set the Division-I single-game scoring record. Not a bad week's work.

He came into the February 7 game against Alabama with two pulled muscles. Late in the contest, he hurt an ankle as well. Despite the injuries, he scored an incredible 47 points in the second half to finish with 69 for the game. Maravich broke the record of 68 points established by Niagara's Calvin Murphy 14 months earlier. (LSU lost the game, 106-104.) His record lasted nearly 21 years, until Kevin Bradshaw of U.S. International scored 72 against Loyola Marymount on Jan. 5, 1991.

Maravich finished his three-time All-American collegiate career with 3,667 points and a 44.2 average, both records that will likely never be broken. His scoring records all were established before the introduction of the three-point shot in the college game. Historians have gone back through game footage from Maravich's career and estimate that had the 3-pointer been in existence in his day, Pistol Pete's career scoring average would have been closer to 57 points per game.

He became a legend in his own time—one of the greatest performers and players in the history of basketball, and arguably the most flamboyant.

"The best showman of all time? I'd have to say Pistol Pete," says former NBA great Isiah Thomas.

"He could do things with a basketball I've never seen anybody do," says NBA Hall of Famer Rick Barry, himself one of the game's great scorers in the '60s and '70s.

After his record-setting college career, Pistol Pete took his act to the NBA's Atlanta Hawks, New Orleans/Utah Jazz, and Boston Celtics. He became a five-time All Pro, a five-time NBA All-Star, and was inducted into the Basketball Hall of Fame in his first year of eligibility. But more than that, Pete Maravich was a trailblazer in the professional ranks, just as he was in college.

"Maravich was unbelievable...he was ahead of his

time," says former L.A. Lakers great Magic Johnson who carried on the Maravich "showtime" style of basketball--and led his team to five NBA titles.

Maravich inspired players like Johnson as he single-handedly thrust basketball into the modern age by putting the emphasis squarely on showmanship and the showman. He was the original ringmaster of big-top basketball; every arena served as his "center ring." No matter who the opponent, no matter what city, when Pete was there, fans were in for quite a show. He brought flare and style to a previously rigid and staid game. He embodied the rebellious, freewheeling nature of his era and seemed to embody young America's antiestablishment spirit. He literally changed the game.

"He opened the minds of a lot of coaches as to how the game could be played. He stepped out on a limb and became a superstar," explains legendary NBA coach Pat Riley.

But even after revolutionizing the NCAA and the NBA, the fire burned inside Maravich to do more. He had an insatiable appetite for basketball. For learning new tricks, for getting better, and for showing the crowds increasingly amazing feats.

Maravich's drive seemed ingrained in his psyche. As a child, he worked on his basketball skills for hours, eschewing other childhood pastimes. His life was all about basketball. He would dribble through the house blindfolded. Dribble while watching a movie in the theater. Dribble while riding his bike or as a passenger in the car. Dribble while he walked to the store. Dribble in the rain. Dribble in the mud. He even slept with his basketball.

"When I was 12 years old," Maravich said, "a reporter came up to me and asked me what I was gonna' do when I grew up—he had seen me play. I said, 'Well, I'm gonna' play pro basketball, get a world championship ring, and make a million dollars.'"

Pistol Pete's boast proved prophetic. He became the first million-dollar athlete, signing a five-year, $1.9 million contract as an NBA rookie in 1970. But he quickly found that the money didn't satisfy him. He hungered for a championship.

Maravich certainly did his part to put his teams into playoff contention. In his ten NBA seasons, he averaged 24.2 points and was named to five All-Star teams. His scoring was legendary at the pro level as well. A February 25,

1977, game against the New York Knicks demonstrated just how Maravich could take over a game.

Midway through the fourth quarter in that game, a New Orleans Jazz teammate told Pistol Pete, "You better get a new firing pin, Pistol, 'cause you're wearing that one out."

But Maravich just kept on firing. By the time he fouled out with 1:18 remaining in the game, he had amassed 68 points, which set a league record for the most points ever for a guard. "I could have scored more," Maravich said later. "I missed a lot of easy shots early in the game."

In breaking the record of 63 points, held by L.A.'s Jerry West in 1962, Maravich hit 26 of 43 field goal attempts and 16 of 19 free throws in the Jazz's 124-107 win at the New Orleans Superdome. He also tallied six assists and six rebounds in his 43 minutes. He scored 17 in the first quarter, 14 in the second, 17 in the third, and 20 in the fourth. "He was phenomenal," said Knicks coach Red Holzman.

Still, despite many stellar performances, Maravich never won an NBA title--thus making him an underachiever in the eyes of many, including himself. Empty and frustrated, he quit the game halfway through the 1979-80 season, at the age of 33.

Tormented by a growing void and a lack of peace in his life, the Pistol looked for fulfillment in astrology, drugs, mysticism, Eastern religions, alcohol, survivalism, nutrition, and even UFOs. At times he considered suicide.

"Nothing satisfied me," said Maravich. "The money didn't. The success didn't. The popularity didn't. The fame didn't. The adulation didn't. There was such an emptiness in my life. I just tried to fill it through basketball, and it didn't do it either. It was so temporal."

But in 1982, Maravich finally found peace through Christian faith. He found purpose, became a committed husband and father—and finally filled the void in his life.

"What I've gained is a joy and a peace in my heart...a purpose in my life that I never had before," Pete said. "That emptiness, that void that was there—is no longer there."

Fittingly, Pistol Pete Maravich died while playing pick-up basketball, on January 5, 1988. At the time of his death, Maravich had no championship ring, but he had peace. An autopsy determined the 40-year-old athlete had been born without the most important artery system that supplies the heart with blood. Normal people have two systems; Maravich had only one. Medical experts said people with similar conditions rarely lived past 20. To have competed at the highest levels in a demanding physical game for three NCAA seasons and 10 more in the NBA--that was next to impossible.

To some, Pete Maravich was a brilliant flame that burned out much too soon. But he lasted long enough to set the basketball world on fire.

Brett Favre celebrates a first-quarter touchdown pass in Super Bowl XXXI.
Don Emmert/AFP/Getty Images

AMAZING ENDURANCE

FAVRE FROM FINISHED

Green Bay Packer quarterback Brett Favre is regarded as one of the most courageous players in NFL history. Favre finished the 2004-2005 season by starting in his 205th consecutive game--a record for quarterbacks. Favre's record is particularly impressive in light of his rough-and-tumble, scrambling style of play--and the emotional turmoil that has dogged him throughout his career.

Indeed, Favre's roller-coaster life reads like a movie script, a script that began in the tiny town of Kiln, Mississippi. Favre's toughness and competitive drive were formed in Kiln under the skillful hands of his coach and father, Irvin. The elder Favre coached baseball and football for 28 years, including serving as high school coach for Brett and his brothers, Scott and Jeff.

Under his father's guidance, Brett developed a reputation as a tough football player. In fact, upon graduation from Kiln's Hancock North Central High School, his only major-college scholarship offer came from Southern Mississippi, which recruited him as a defensive back, not a quarterback.

However, by the time he graduated from Southern Miss (in 1991), he had set 18 school records, as a QB. It was during his college career that he first demonstrated his legendary resilience. Prior to his senior year, he ran his truck into a tree, suffering a severe concussion, a broken vertebrae, and serious internal injuries--which necessitated the removal of 30 inches of his intestine. Just two months after the accident, Favre took to the field, leading the Golden Eagles to an upset win over powerhouse Alabama.

Despite such heroics, Favre still had doubters among NFL scouts and coaches. He wasn't chosen in the first round of the 1991 draft, slipping to the second round, when the Atlanta Falcons picked him. He played only two games for the Falcons before being shipped to the Packers.

The next season, Favre began establishing his legend in Green Bay. In a game against Cincinnati, Packer starter Don

Majkowski went down with a fourth-quarter injury. With his team trailing 17-3, Favre entered the game and rallied the Packers around him. Using his athleticism and strong arm, Favre led his team to a thrilling 24-23 comeback win and was named the starting QB the following week.

And since earning that starting job, he hasn't been out of the lineup--despite broken thumbs, injured knees, twisted ankles, bruised hips and ribs, and multiple concussions.

Favre was the NFL's MVP in 1995 and again in '96, when he tossed an NFC single-season record 39 touchdown passes. That same season, Favre helped the Pack reclaim the glory it held in the 1960s—leading his team to the NFL championship in Super Bowl XXXI. Green Bay's appearance in the big game ended a 29-year drought. In 1997, he won an unprecedented third straight league MVP award and once again led his team to the Super Bowl. At the end of the 2004 season, Favre stood second in NFL history in career touchdown passes, and third in passing yards, completions, and wins by a quarterback. He had also been named to eight Pro Bowls.

Throughout his career, Favre has endeared himself to fans around the league who view him as an "everyman" who made it big. Nowhere was his relationship with fans more special than in Green Bay, where he became a symbol of the area's blue-collar work ethic and never-say-die attitude.

"No player in the NFL identifies with, or is more closely linked to, a specific team like Brett Favre is to the Green Bay Packers," explains Packers coach Mike Sherman. "He embodies the spirit and character of Packer fans everywhere. I do not think there is a player in the NFL that experiences a relationship with the fans like Brett Favre does. That is very, very special."

But Favre's success on the field hasn't come without its challenges off it. Midway through his career, as his play steadily improved, his personal life crumbled. He has battled addictions to alcohol and painkillers. By 1999, his addictive personality had nearly cost him his family.

"I was still drinking, and I was not the husband, was not the father that I needed to be," Favre recalls. "I was getting older too, and it [football] wasn't as much fun. If I quit drinking, what do I do? I was scared of that. My wife said, 'Either you quit drinking or we're gone.' And I said 'Okay. I'm going to quit.'"

And so he did.

Clean from the substance-abuse problems that had hounded him, Favre learned to balance football with his personal life. He learned that true strength isn't found in a bottle. Renewed, he attacked life and his career with an enhanced passion, unaware of how much he would need to depend on that new strength and toughness in the years ahead.

On Sunday, December 21, 2003, Favre's father, Irvin, suffered a severe heart attack while driving his car, resulting in a fatal accident. Favre had lost his father and his first coach.

That same night, on the eve of an important Monday night game, in what was likely his most difficult test, Favre addressed his teammates in an emotional team meeting. He told them that despite his pain, he would not abandon his football family. His teammates already knew Favre was willing to play through broken bones. Now they saw he would play with a broken heart.

"I've never seen a leader or a player like Brett in my career, and I'm pretty sure that no one else in this locker room has either," noted then-teammate Wesley Walls. "Just getting up in front of the team at such a horrible and difficult time in his life really showed he cared about us. That was something I'll never forget."

A grieving Favre took the field the next day for a

Monday night game against the Oakland Raiders. Under the intense glare of the national spotlight, Favre proved once again why he is considered the most courageous quarterback ever. He inspired his teammates with one of the greatest performances of his storied career, passing for 311 yards and four touchdowns in the first half alone. He finished the game with 399 yards passing, leading his team to a 41-7 rout. It was perhaps the signature moment of his career, epitomizing Favre's true character and heart.

"I knew that my dad would have wanted me to play," Favre said following the game. "I love him so much, and I love this game. It's meant a great deal to me, to my dad, to my family, and I didn't expect this kind of performance. But I know he was watching tonight."

"What Brett did was immeasurable. Not a lot of guys can put that [grief] on the back burner and go out there and accomplish the things he accomplished for himself, his team, and Green Bay," receiver Antonio Freeman said in the aftermath. "You can't measure it. You can't put a price on it. I don't know how he did it, but he did it."

The following week, just four days after burying his father, Favre led the Packers to a 31-3 season-ending victory and a spot in the playoffs.

The adversity continued for Favre the following season. In October of 2004, his wife, Deanna, was diagnosed with breast cancer. Facing chemotherapy treatments, Deanna displayed an attitude like her husband's, refusing to be defeated. Brett Favre became his wife's biggest supporter, once shaving his head in a sign of support after Deanna had begun to lose her hair due to treatments.

On the field, the toughest man in the NFL carried on, with his wife's blessing. He faced adversity like an oncoming blitz, stiff-arming, sidestepping, ducking his head, and charging forward. While many wondered if retirement was near, Favre was simply enjoying playing the game.

"I love to play the game. I still feel like I can play at a high level," he explained. "But there were other issues—not just me—that I had to deal with. My wife said, 'Hey, go back and play,' and that made my decision much easier.…When it counts, I still think I'm the best, and that keeps me kicking myself in the butt and being not quite ready to leave yet."

In early 2005, Deanna completed her chemotherapy treatments. Shortly thereafter, Favre announced that he was returning to the Packers for his 15th NFL season.

"I realize that I'm doing something that I can do for only a small time in my life," Favre says, "and I might as well enjoy it as long as I can. Before you know it, it's gone. I'm one of the few guys who, I think, is aware of what I'm able to do and the surroundings and what this means. Some guys—before they know it, they're gone and they [say], 'If I could have just held on to the moment.' I'm doing that, and I'm holding on for as long as I can."